REACH EVERY ATHLETE

A Guide to Coaching Players with Hidden Disabilities and Conditions

Christopher Stanley, PhD, CMPC
Associate Research Faculty
Quantitative Methods and Innovation
Florida State University
Tallahassee, Florida

Timothy Baghurst, PhD, RFSA
Director, FSU COACH
Professor, College of Education
Florida State University
Tallahassee, Florida

World Headquarters
Jones & Bartlett Learning
25 Mall Road
Burlington, MA 01803
978-443-5000
info@jblearning.com
www.jblearning.com

Jones & Bartlett Learning books and products are available through most bookstores and online booksellers. To contact Jones & Bartlett Learning directly, call 800-832-0034, fax 978-443-8000, or visit our website, www.jblearning.com.

Substantial discounts on bulk quantities of Jones & Bartlett Learning publications are available to corporations, professional associations, and other qualified organizations. For details and specific discount information, contact the special sales department at Jones & Bartlett Learning via the above contact information or send an email to specialsales@jblearning.com.

Production Credits
Vice President, Product Management: Marisa R. Urbano
Vice President, Product Operations: Christine Emerton
Director of Product Management: Matthew Kane
Product Manager: Whitney Fekete
Content Strategist: Carol Brewer Guerrero
Product Coordinator: Samantha Gillespie
Project Manager: Kristen Rogers
Senior Project Specialist: Dan Stone
Director of Marketing: Andrea DeFronzo
Senior Digital Project Specialist: Angela Dooley
VP, Manufacturing and Inventory Control: Therese Connell
Composition: Exela Technologies
Project Management: Exela Technologies
Cover Design: Kristin Parker
Text Design: Michael O'Donnell
Content Services Manager: Colleen Lamy
Media Development Editor: Faith Brosnan
Rights & Permissions Manager: John Rusk
Rights Specialist: Benjamin Roy
Cover Image (Title Page, Part Opener, Chapter Opener): © miodrag ignjatovic/Getty Images.
Printing and Binding: McNaughton & Gunn

Library of Congress Cataloging-in-Publication Data
Library of Congress Control Number: 2021921316

6048

Printed in the United States of America
26 25 24 23 22 10 9 8 7 6 5 4 3 2 1

About SHAPE America

SHAPE America – Society of Health and Physical Educators serves as the voice for 200,000+ health and physical education professionals across the United States. The organization's extensive community includes a diverse membership of health and physical educators, as well as advocates, supporters, and 50+ state affiliate organizations.

© Klaus Vedfelt/DigitalVision/Getty Images

Since its founding in 1885, the organization has defined excellence in physical education. For decades, SHAPE America's National Standards for K-12 Physical Education have served as the foundation for well-designed physical education programs across the country. Additionally, the organization helped develop and owns the National Health Education Standards.

SHAPE America provides programs, resources and advocacy to support health and physical educators at every grade level as they prepare all students to lead a healthy, physically active life. The organization's newest program — health. moves. minds.® — helps teachers and schools incorporate social and emotional learning so students can thrive physically *and* emotionally.

Our Vision

A nation where all children are prepared to lead healthy, physically active lives.

Our Mission

To advance professional practice and promote research related to health and physical education, physical activity, dance and sport.

© FatCamera/E+/Getty Images

To learn more, visit
www.shapeamerica.org

Brief Contents

Contents

Acknowledgments

SHAPE America Acknowledgments

Thomas Lawson, SHAPE America Vice President of Marketing, Membership and Publications

SHAPE America Publications Advisory Committee

Holly Alperin, University of New Hampshire
Jayne Greenburg, US Department of Health and Human Services
Louis Harrison, The University of Texas at Austin
Brent Heidorn, University of West Georgia
Minsoo Kang, The University of Mississippi
Pamela Kulinna, Arizona State University
K. Andrew R. Richards, University of Illinois at Urbana-Champaign
Kristi Roth, University of Wisconsin-Stevens Point

About the Authors

Christopher Stanley is research faculty at Florida State University with academic and professional backgrounds in Sport Psychology and Developmental Psychology. Professionally, he has been a collegiate coach (Florida A & M University; University of Illinois-Chicago) and Psychology faculty at Winston-Salem State University and Florida Gulf Coast University. He is involved in numerous projects related to education, performance, and learning disabilities. He has authored a lifespan development textbook along with numerous peer-reviewed journal articles, white papers, and book chapters broadly related to the psychosocial aspects of sport participation and performance, as well as educational issues and outcomes. Much of his scholarship and writing is relevant for coaching audiences. He is a sport psychology consultant with a variety of athletes and coaches, including with USA Track and Field, traveling with several national teams.

Timothy Baghurst is the Director of FSU COACH: Interdisciplinary Center for Athletic Coaching at Florida State University. His doctorate is in physical education and he holds other graduate degrees in education, kinesiology, and sport and exercise psychology. Tim is widely published across sport psychology, physical education, and coaching. He has authored several books in addition to having authored over 100 peer-reviewed publications. He has served as the Chair of the editorial board of *Strategies* in addition to working with many other journals.

He consults and coaches for several professional and amateur athletes and coaches. More information can be found at www.timbaghurst.com.

Contributor

Joanne P. McCallie, MBA, BA
Former Duke University and Michigan State University Women's Basketball Head Coach
Author: Secret Warrior/Choice, Not Chance
CoachP4Life/Foundation
Durham, North Carolina

Reviewers

James Barry, PhD, CAPE
Assistant Professor
Salisbury University
Salisbury, Maryland

Erika Bonadio, EdD
Assistant Professor and Chair of Department, Exercise Science
Salem College
Winston-Salem, North Carolina

R. Michael Cathey, PhD
Associate Professor
University of Tennessee – Southern
Pulaski, Tennessee

DeAnne Davis Brooks, EdD, CSCS, CE-P
UNC Greensboro
Greensboro, North Carolina

Scott Douglas, PhD, CAPE
Associate Professor
University of Northern Colorado
Greeley, Colorado

Kelli J. Esteves
Professor of Education
College of Education, Butler University
Indianapolis, Indiana

Fritz I. Ettl Rodriguez
Assistant Professor, Human Movement and Health Science Education
College of Education, Butler University
Indianapolis, Indiana

Anthony Girardi, MA, CSCS
Instructor
William Paterson University
Wayne, New Jersey

Meghan Halbrook, PhD
Director, Master of Arts in Coaching and Sport Leadership
Randolph College
Lynchburg, Virginia

Amy D. Linder, PhD
Assistant Professor
North Carolina Central University
Durham, North Carolina

Fay Nielsen, PhD
Associate Professor
Fresno Pacific University
Fresno, California

Chad Payn, EdD
Assistant Professor of Exercise Science, Sports & Recreation
Oklahoma Baptist University
Shawnee, Oklahoma

Jamie Robbins, PhD, CMPC
Professor
Methodist University
Fayetteville, North Carolina

Paula J. Scraba, PhD, OSF
Associate Professor
St. Bonaventure University
St. Bonaventure, New York

Kathryn Shea, PhD
Associate Professor
Director, Sport Management Program
Fisher College
Boston, Massachusetts

Tammy Sheehy, PhD
Assistant Professor
Bridgewater College
Bridgewater, Virginia

Anthony S. Smith, PhD, CSCS*D, NSCA-CPT*D, TSAC-F*D
Associate Professor of Physical Education
Charleston Southern University
Charleston, South Carolina

Brad Strand, PhD
North Dakota State University
Fargo, North Dakota

Sandy Wilson, EdD
Associate Professor of Kinesiology
Coastal Carolina University
Conway, South Carolina

Andrea Woodson-Smith, PhD
Professor
North Carolina Central University
Durham, North Carolina

Foreword

This is not the first book we have written. But, perhaps, it is the most important of them all. Authors of nonfiction typically search for a gap in the knowledge base and seek to fill it. This is what we have done, not because we desperately wanted to write a book, but because we both have firsthand experience working with athletes who have had hidden disabilities and conditions (HDCs), some of which were undiagnosed at that time. Knowing that there was something going on, but not quite being able to pinpoint exactly what, was incredibly frustrating. It made the individual hard to coach, because while we might suspect a problem, without a clear understanding of what that problem was, there were no guidelines or plan to help that athlete and the whole team. Understand that a difficulty with one athlete transcends that athlete and affects everyone around.

The primary purpose of this book is to expose you, the coach, to the myriad of HDCs that might exist within your athletic population. Of course, we cannot cover all of them, but we cover many of the more common ones that might arise in sports settings. Awareness is the first step in making adjustments, and we want to make you more aware in your coaching. From that position, you can differentiate your coaching to best meet the needs of your athletes in your situation. While we do provide some vignettes to highlight each area, they are just vignettes, and your situation will be very specific to you. Therefore, it is important to take this material and apply it to your unique setting.

Joanne P. McCallie, former collegiate NCAA Division I basketball coach and now advocate and speaker on mental health, wrote the introduction to this book. We asked her specifically because of her own experiences; as a coach in her mid-20s, she was diagnosed with bipolar disorder. There are some important lessons in this fact. Namely, coaches may be struggling with HDCs, and we should not assume that HDCs are diagnosed during youth. They can occur at any age!

We must also recognize that athletes may not come forward with their struggles. McCallie stated that she fears what an HDC diagnosis might mean to a coach's career or the stigma that might be attached to them. Not surprisingly; therefore, coaches are likely to hide or suppress any hint of a problem. Now, transition this logic to an athlete who might be worried about playing time, scholarships, contracts, sponsorships, and so on. As a coach, do not expect athletes or parents to quickly volunteer information that they might fear would impact these other variables. Therefore, as a coach, you must be thoughtful, observant, inquisitive, and be open to the possibility that an athlete may be struggling with an HDC. Without that openness, the odds of a condition being brought forward are highly unlikely.

And so, we begin, recognizing that our book is not an encyclopedia of HDCs, but that it provides the starting point for the transformational coach who puts their athletes' health and well-being above all else. If you have experiences to share or have questions, reach out to us! We want to hear from you, and we hope that the content to follow changes lives in a positive way.

—**Chris Stanley** and **Tim Baghurst**

Hidden Disabilities and Conditions Awareness

CHAPTER 1

Introduction

By **Joanne McCallie**, Former Duke University and Michigan State University Women's Basketball Head Coach

Drs. Chris Stanley and Tim Baghurst provide an historical, thorough, specific, and inclusive educational book that explains the parameters and processes that help coaches reach and support all athletes with hidden disabilities and conditions. This book examines the broader-based concepts relative to coaching in an increasingly informed and diverse world of sport. From specific learning disorders (like dyslexia), to Autism, to Attention Deficit Hyperactivity Disorder (ADHD), along with many other physical and mental conditions that challenge the athlete, are researched and presented in an easy to understand and applicable format.

It is important to ask the coaching community as a whole to change its perspectives and grow regarding its perceptions and understanding of disabilities and conditions in sports. As Stanley and Baghurst clearly state, "Disability is an umbrella term covering impairments, activity limitations, and participant restrictions." Therefore, coaches must be pivotal in fostering an environment of clarity, support, motivation, inclusion, fairness, and leadership. They must give careful thought to the positive experiences of each athlete. Finding that balance, in order to reach every athlete, with hidden and sometimes not so hidden disabilities and conditions, is the ultimate challenge of those who choose the multifaceted field of coaching.

The positive short-term experiences combined with the richer long-term effects are reasons for how and why coaches should find ways to identify and support athletes who experience disabilities and conditions. Constraints are ever-present and often intimidating, as legal boundaries exist for privacy and protection of each athlete. Therefore, the relationships among coaches, athletes, and often their parents or guardians provide a unique opportunity to communicate and negotiate the expectations and nature of a coach's philosophy. The action of negotiating is a challenging task because the coach must manage and work within the diverse nature of coaching where many unique situations and athletes exist.

As often is the case with athletes, their desire, and sometimes the desire of their parents, for a meaningful and fulfilling experience requires the coach to wear many hats, balancing and adapting to information that becomes critical in each unique situation. In this way, the coaching craft has morphed into physical assessments and role determination, bound by the parameters of best practices, relative to the strengths and challenges of each athlete. The process-driven craft of effective coaching focuses specifically on the talents and limits of each participant. Therefore, close examination of each person and their own unique situation becomes critical in integrating the realities of disabilities with the opportunities for very positive outcomes. However daunting, this process-driven approach, where outcomes are not the key focus, leads to success at all levels of coaching and a heightened experience for the athlete as well.

As coaches lead within the context of each situation, the concepts of immediacy, intelligence, and intensity require discussion. Regardless of the constraints, coaches must be *immediate* with each situation and carve a pathway for each participant to thrive. Individual sports differ from team sports, of course, but the concept of teaching immediacy comes into play relative to communication and direct strategies that foster a healthy and inclusive environment. *Intelligence* speaks to the communication and outreach necessary among parents, athletes, and coaches to share information. Coaches must understand an athlete's limits while also being able to teach and demand excellence from them as appropriate, thereby providing an authentic experience for each athlete. *Intensity* is also part of the equation, as the athlete's ability to participate at the highest level of effort and focus cannot be compromised during the process of individual discovery and performance.

Through critical details and study of the many variants within disabilities conditions, this book clearly identifies the many possible challenges that can be a part of the athlete/coaching dynamic. Mental and physical health both work in concert to bring out the best in all of us. The appropriateness and direct approach of these writings serves the complicated, but more informed, society of today. We are making great progress with understanding the nuances of brain and body health. The thorough nature of this writing offers the reader and researcher a template of knowledge to expand the horizons of athlete participation beyond the scope of what has been possible in the past.

The role of coaches and parents is also a relationship of trust and shared information that can maximize all outcomes relative to positive experiences in sports. Technical study of sport dynamics and disabilities, combined with the psychosocial conditions and mental health literacy and trauma-informed coaching, is the greater challenge for all. This shapes the future of coaching as an even more unique craft. This book provides research, information, stories, implications, and concise writing that tackles a large amount of information while giving direction and guidance to all parties charged with creating a diverse, competitive, positive, and character-developing experience.

Participation in sports, whether at a high level of performance or recreational, will always include unique disabilities and conditions that coaches will experience. The sports arena and the craft of coaching is enhanced by learning and adapting to new data and information. Stanley and Baghurst clearly articulate the methodology and creative structure to help identify and support athletes with hidden disabilities and conditions. This content aids in welcoming all athletes to be part of and succeed at sports.

CHAPTER 2

Awareness and Planning

Disability Sport

The history of disability sport can be found across all ages, sport types, and levels of competition. This may include sport and fitness opportunities in community and recreational centers and organizations, public and private school athletics, colleges and universities, clubs, and elite and professional sport organizations.

According to the *World Report on Disability*, approximately 15% of the world's population (about 1 billion individuals) experience some form of disability (Wylie, McAllister, Davidson, & Marshall, 2013). In the United States, about 57 million individuals have some form of disability (Martin, 2017). Disabilities may range from those that are congenital to those that are acquired; and also include those that are hidden to those that are visible in nature.

Persons with a disability are defined as those "…who have long-term physical, mental, intellectual, or sensory conditions which in interaction with various barriers may hinder their full and effective participation in society on an equal basis with others." (United Nations, 2006). This definition does not just reflect the biological nature of a condition but also reflects the discriminatory, marginalizing, and challenging physical and social environments people may experience (Martin, 2017). The World Health Organization (WHO; 2016) similarly defines disability but also considers forms of activity and participation restrictions:

> "Disability is an umbrella term, covering impairments, activity limitations, and participation restrictions. An impairment in a problem in body function or structure; activity limitation is difficulty encountered by an individual in executing a task or action; while a participation restriction is a problem experienced by an individual in involvement in life situations."

Moving forward in this text, the term *condition* will be used. Above and beyond how the term *impairment* is described above, condition more broadly captures some additional topics covered in the book (e.g., diabetes, asthma, athlete triad).

There has been a great deal of legislation to promote access to and participation in exercise, recreation, and sport for people with disabilities.

Several core pieces of legislation have advanced accessibility and inclusive practices in educational and sport areas. For instance, in 1973, Section 504 of the Rehabilitation Act ensured equal access and opportunities for those with disabilities to programs, services, and venues. These included national parks and federally funded fitness initiatives. In 1990, passage of the Americans with Disabilities Act (ADA) explicitly banned discrimination based on disability in employment and education. The ADA also required accessibility (i.e., entry ramps, bathroom facilities, locker rooms) for newly constructed buildings and transportation systems. Also in 1990, the Individuals with Disabilities Education Act (IDEA) was passed, which sought to standardize education for students with disabilities, including participation in physical education. These legislative acts have helped facilitate accessible spaces and inclusive practices (Mascarinas & Blauwet, 2018).

While coaches may be limited in how much of the "architectural" items they can quickly secure or make accessible to individual athletes, there are many ways they can be an integral part of making athletes with disabilities feel included on their teams. Coaches can also help support the athletic development and well-being of these athletes. In other words, coaches are important in making *inclusive sport*, where people of all abilities and interests can participate. Sport represents a context in which adaptations occur to enhance participation and promote inclusion. The degree to which persons with disabilities are included can range from general lack of inclusive opportunities to full inclusion. Coaches can examine where they feel their team, sport, or organization falls along this continuum of inclusion.

Forber-Pratt and Lyew (2019) offered a continuum of inclusion relevant for sport. On one end of the continuum, inclusion appears 'forced' and the spaces shared by people with and without disabilities lack any real attempts for accessibility and inclusivity. Moving along on the continuum are instances in which partial inclusion exists, either for certain disability groups, or certain sports. However, complete inclusion and accessibility are still lacking. On the other end of the spectrum are athletic contexts and spaces with full inclusion opportunities for all individuals, representing all disability groups. Even further on this end of the inclusion continuum is where inclusion is a 'norm' in society.

Movement toward making sport accessible for everyone has resulted in many organizations and events, including the Parapan American Games, Deaflympics, Paralympics, Special Olympics, Invictus Games, Warrior Games, and Warfighter Sports. These often have distinct criteria and categories for involvement. For example, in the references section at the end of this chapter is the webpage for the Paralympic classification standards.

While the International Paralympic Committee allows for vision (which reaches a minimum criteria level) to qualify one as a Paralympic athlete and sport, the other conditions covered in this book in and of themselves would not necessarily qualify one for para-sport. However, they may still require the coach to consider how to adapt the sport environment to meet that athlete. In many of these cases, the disabilities and conditions permit full inclusion, although the athletes and coaches must still negotiate their participation and performance related to their social, cognitive, motor, and muscular skills and abilities.

Hidden Disabilities and Conditions

This book is written for athletes with a particular range of disabilities and conditions (and their coaches) in mind. As the title of the book indicates, the term *hidden disability* and conditions (HDCs) is used throughout. Some of these include learning disabilities (dyslexia, dyscalculia), autism spectrum, and ADHD. Also, a variety of sensory or other conditions that impact musculature, motor movement, or health are included.

It is important to note that this book is *not* a clinical guide for coaches to make (even informal) diagnoses of their athletes. The disabilities and conditions covered in the following chapters, along with typical observable symptoms, are intended to give coaches some reference points. These reference points can be used to help coaches think through reasons why respective athletes may be experiencing challenges based upon observations.

There are undoubtedly many instances of HDCs in sport settings in which the coach simply will not know that the disabilities and conditions are present ... either because the athlete has never been diagnosed in a medical setting or because they have been diagnosed and choose not to tell their coach(es) or teammate(s). They may personally choose not to let others know for any number reasons including fear of embarrassment, reduction in playing time, unwanted attention, or isolation. In that vein, the authors of the book cannot make assumptions about the level of *disclosure*—or what the athlete has informed others of regarding a disability or condition—that occurs between a coach and athlete. That likely depends on many factors, including the conditions, the severity of the symptoms, the athlete's comfort level with the coach, the athlete's chronological age and athletic level, and so on.

© Fuse/Thinkstock.

The authors encourage coaches to promote and model openness, honesty, and concern for their athletes. Such a team climate may promote disclosure (if the athlete feels so inclined) and also collaborative dialogue and problem solving. With that in mind, when reading the chapters of this book and when taking things learned back to athletes, we encourage coaches to:

- Be willing to learn (from athletes, parents and guardians, medical professionals, and others).
- Be unafraid to acknowledge when they don't know something.
- Ask questions from athletes and others (parents, guardians, medical staff).
- Ask the athlete if they are unsure of what they can or cannot do in the sport.
- Be an ally for all athletes.
- Be open to trying new techniques they think may work based upon what they know about their athlete(s).
- Be confident in their coaching abilities and their desire to make an inclusive environment (Forber-Pratt, 2020).

Together, coaches can take steps, even small ones, to move their sport environment toward a more inclusive space that is athletically and mentally healthy for a wide range of individuals, including those with HDCs.

Communication and Planning

Coaches may rely on caregivers and families for support in many cases. When needing to communicate with families and caregivers about children and athletes, it may be helpful to approach it from a "partnership" perspective. While you maintain different roles and responsibilities in the child's life, coaches are uniquely important to children and adolescents, particularly when they are with the athlete over seasons and years.

When noticing something in an athlete, a coach may initiate communication with the family first. Sometimes this is made easier if the coach had established prior connection, whether an introductory meeting at the beginning of a season or an email. Coaches may develop a baseline level of communication, letting families know how their child is doing. If something arises that causes concern (such as any of the issues or symptoms covered in this book), coaches will benefit from being as timely as possible by not letting too much time elapse between the observation(s) and the first attempt at contact. Thereafter, families may appreciate follow through and follow-up. If there was an agreed-upon decision concerning the child, coaches can let the family know how it appears to be working. While the *Zero to Three* organization focuses primarily on care of infants and toddlers, they offer some useful tips on communicating with family members and caregivers:

- Use "I" statements when speaking to caregivers about their child(ren)
  - "I observed..."
  - "I wanted your feedback..."
  - "I have an idea that may improve your child's experience..."
- Ask for the family member's advice and perspective.
- Speak to the child's strengths as well as areas that could use improvement.
- Compromise when necessary.
- Check up.

The above will demonstrate a partnership approach and concern for the youth athlete. Another benefit of establishing healthy communication is that it may prompt disclosure of the HDCs (if disclosure had not occurred already) or it may facilitate attempts from the family to seek professional guidance for their child. Another benefit is that families may help establish individualized athlete plans for coaches. These plans could be in terms of accommodation ideas to meet the athlete's needs, including transitional activities for those entering sport and team environments for the first time.

These plans could also be in relation to possibilities where medical situations arise. Specific medical advice is beyond the scope of this book. However, certain items to consider are drawn out in subsequent chapters, offering a "checklist" of sorts for coaches to refer to when setting up or modifying practices, as well as traveling to competitions, to protect the health and safety of athletes who may have HDCs. Coaches can help athletes and their families establish preventative measures in and around their sport environment. As with physical health and movement, steps can be taken to prevent injuries. However, in the case of more serious injuries, a coach benefits from knowing where to find the nearest medical professional to stabilize the situation and otherwise have a cell phone nearby to call 9-1-1. Similarly, with some serious symptoms and situations outlined in this book (e.g., diabetes, asthma, allergies, mental health), coaches will benefit from knowing where the closest people and resources are who would be able to treat the athlete or call 9-1-1.

Summary

- Approximately 15% of the world's population experience some form of disability.
- Coaches are important in making *inclusive sport*, where people of all abilities and interests can participate. There are many ways in which they can be an integral part of making athletes with disabilities feel included on their teams.
- Coaches can also help support the athletic development and well-being of these athletes.
- Many of the HDCs covered in this book may require the coach to consider how to adapt the sport environment to accommodate that athlete.
- Coaches may model openness, honesty, and concern for their athletes in creating a healthy and inclusive team climate.

Questions for Consideration

1. What percentage of the world's population experiences some form of disability?
2. What is the difference between the terms "disability" and "impairment/condition?"
3. Inclusion is an important term. Explain how your primary sport provides opportunities for athletes with HDCs.
4. We encourage coaches to do several things when reading this book. Which item do you think will be the most challenging for you? Why?
5. Coaches may be the first to identify HDCs. What concerns you the most about approaching the athlete or parent about your concerns? Explain.

References

Forber-Pratt, A. J. (2020). *Disability sport: A parallel push for inclusion* [Conference presentation]. Association for Applied Sport Psychology 2020 Conference, Virtual.

Forber-Pratt, A. J., & Lyew, D. A. (2020). A model case: Specialized group home for girls with disabilities in India. *Child and Adolescent Social Work Journal*, *37*, 315–327. https://doi.org/10.1007/s10560-019-00633-8

Martin, J. J. (2017). *Handbook of disability sport and exercise psychology*. Oxford University Press.

Mascarinas, A., & Blauwet, C. (2018). Policy and advocacy initiatives to promote the benefits of sports participation for individuals with disability. In J. De Luigi (Ed.), *Adaptive sports medicine* (pp. 371–384). Springer. https://doi.org/10.1007/978-3-319-56568-2_30

International Paralympic Committee. (2016). Paralympic classifications. https://www.paralympic.org/ International_Standard_for_Eligible_ConditionConditions_1.pdf

United Nations. (2006). Convention on the Rights of Persons with Disabilities and Optional Protocol. https://www.un.org/disabilities/documents/convention/convoptprot-e.pdf

World Health Organization (n.d.). Disability. https://www.who.int/topics/disabilities/en

Wylie, K., McAllister, L., Davidson, B., & Marshall, J. (2013). Changing practice: Implications of the World Report on Disability for responding to communication disability in under-served populations. *International Journal of Speech-Language Pathology*, *15*(1), 1–13.

Zero to Three. (n.d.). *How to communicate with parents*. https://www.zerotothree.org/resources/92-how-to-communicate-with-parents

PART 2

Hidden Disabilities

CHAPTER 3

Specific Learning Disorders (Dyslexia, Dysgraphia, Dyscalculia)

VIGNETTE Part One

Coach Halliwell called a timeout with 13 seconds to go. It was a good timeout. Down by one, 46–47, her players quickly walked to the sideline for instructions. With a two- or three-point shot available, she knew the opponents were going to have to plan and worry about what she would be drawing up.

Halliwell's players huddled around her as she pulled the lid off of her marker. There was a lot of noise around the gym, and it felt a bit chaotic, but she tried to remain composed.

"Alright everyone, this is it. This is where we want to be; the ball's in our hands and we have a chance to win it. So, here's what we're going to do. Keisha, I want you to inbound to the most open player. If you can get it to Lauren immediately, then do it, because I want Lauren to take the last shot."

Halliwell looked up at Lauren and made eye contact as she said this. Lauren nodded confidently, which is what Halliwell wanted to see. Lauren was her best player, and when it's crunch time, you want your best player with the ball.

Halliwell continued. "So, Keisha inbounds to the most open player. Whichever one of you gets it needs to work the ball to Lauren, which may need you to set a screen. You have plenty of time, 13 seconds, so don't force anything. She will get open. Keisha, what's your role and the team's role?"

"Inbound to the most open player and then we work the ball to Lauren if it isn't her in the first place, she replied."

"Good," said Halliwell, checking her instructions for understanding. "Okay, Lauren, you've got this. Take the shot you're most comfortable with. You can drive to the basket or pull up, depending on the look you get. I know how good you are at both. But, don't shoot unless there are less than 2 or 3 seconds max on the clock, okay? We don't want to give them a chance to get the ball back down the court."

"Got it, Coach," Lauren responded. "Less than 3 seconds."

"Alright ladies, let's go and execute like we know we can."

The team broke up and headed to their preplanned positions on the floor. As the whistle blew, Lauren darted past her opponent and Keisha passed her the ball. Coach

Halliwell breathed a little easier now that Lauren was in control, but her heart was still pounding. Lauren moved her way to the top of the key and waited. The clock slowly ticked, and ticked, and ticked while everyone waited for Lauren to explode into action. But, to Halliwell's shock, Lauren began her approach to the basket with 7 seconds left. Jinking left, then pulling right, Lauren stopped on a dime and pulled up for the jumper. Everyone held their breath as the ball arced through the air before banging the rim and then slowly dropping in for two points.

As the ball dropped, her players jumped up and down in celebration, but Coach Halliwell looked back to the clock. Five seconds remained, which was plenty of time for their opponents to take that lead once again. Why hadn't Lauren followed her instructions?

Forms, Definitions, and Prevalence

Specific learning disorders (SLDs) relate to a range of difficulties in learning and application of academic skills. Given the focus on difficulties with academic skills, SLDs tend to be in areas typically found in school, including reading, writing, and mathematics. While SLDs tend to show in early childhood, they are not something someone will necessarily "outgrow." Individuals with SLDs may learn to accommodate these challenges by using different strategies.

Although learning difficulties may be more severe and impact more than one area (reading, writing, and/or mathematics) having an SLD does not necessarily mean someone suffers in other mental (creative, imaginative) or physical (motor skills, sport) ways. Students with a documented SLD may perform, or outperform, their peers in other areas not impacted by the disability. In fact, the term twice exceptional (or 2e) is used to describe students who are intellectually gifted and have a SLD. Among elementary school students, approximately 5 to 15% of children have an SLD. The most common SLD is dyslexia, with some estimates being as high as 1 in 5 students having this learning disorder.

Reading—Dyslexia

There are many potential reasons why individuals are at risk of not attaining full literacy skills. They may be at risk because they are English language learners, struggling to learn literacy skills in two languages simultaneously (Gersten, 1996); the low performance on literacy tests may be because they are struggling to learn a language rather than an indicator of an underlying disability. They may be at risk because they move from school to school regularly, and each move has significant transition adjustments that interfere with academic development, including literacy skills. However, for the most part, students may be at risk for not attaining full literacy skills because of a disability, including dyslexia. Usually, this is not because of one single cause but a variety of reasons (Snowling, 2012). Multiple risk factors may interact with each other to make literacy problems more pronounced than if only one risk factor were present (Muter & Snowling, 2009).

Dyslexia is commonly understood as a brain-based learning disability that specifically impairs a person's ability to read (Peterson & Pennington, 2015). In addition to its impact upon reading skills, dyslexia has been linked with decreases

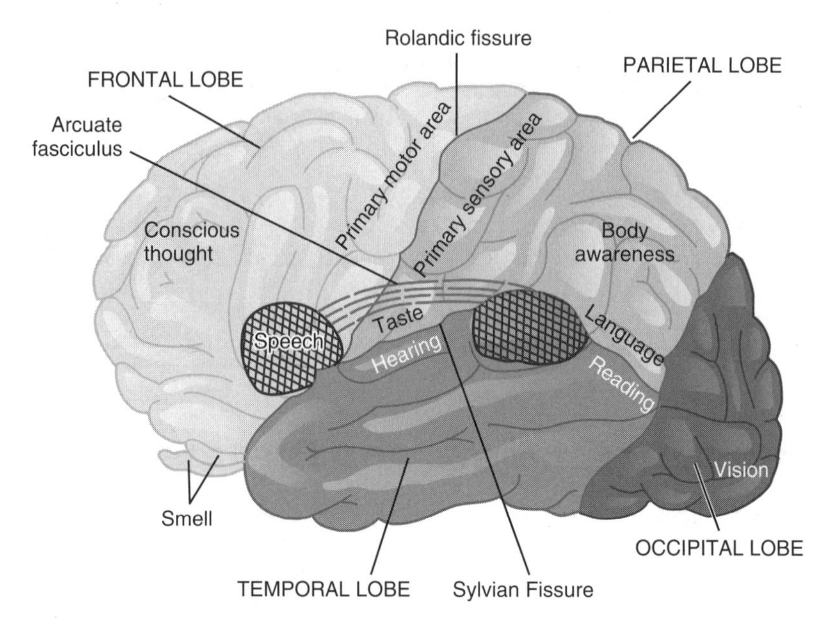

Figure 3.1 Regions of the brain.

in self-esteem and amount of time reading outside of school contexts; this means that the gap in reading ability, vocabulary, and background knowledge is likely to increase over time compared with those without dyslexia (Undheim, 2003). States increasingly use the International Dyslexia Association definition of dyslexia:

> Essentially, dyslexia is a specific learning disability with a neurological basis. Individuals with dyslexia may demonstrate difficulty with accurate and/or fluent word recognition, spelling, and word decoding abilities. These difficulties are often unexpected in relation to other cognitive and intellectual capabilities. For a full definition and description of dyslexia, readers may visit the website of the International Dyslexia Association (listed in the resources at the end of this chapter).

As shown in **Figure 3.1**, the differences in brain regions for those with dyslexia are primarily in the left hemisphere of the brain—the "language dominant" hemisphere—which is linked to many language and reading capabilities.

Writing—Dysgraphia

Dysgraphia may be identified or diagnosed as an SLD involving difficulties with written expression. Individuals with dysgraphia may have typical literacy skills and development but have difficulty in a set of skills related to transcribing information, including handwriting, typing, and spelling. These difficulties may be viewed in frequent misspelling of words, messy handwriting, difficulty in forming letters and spacing words correctly on a page, or writing in a straight line. There also may be difficulties in holding, maneuvering, or applying correct pressure with writing utensils in handwriting tasks.

Numerical Information and Mathematics—Dyscalculia

Individuals with dyscalculia have difficulty working with numbers and working with concepts such as "smaller" or "larger." Additional problem areas may include counting, recalling mathematical facts (like multiplication tables), calculating, using mathematical symbols and commands, reading a clock, working with money transactions, or holding numbers in their head while solving problems. As one ages, this could translate into difficulties managing time, cooking, or shopping.

As with other SLDs, dyscalculia does not imply a problem with intelligence or lack of effort. Unfortunately, dyscalculia can often be overlooked and attributed to someone being "bad at math." As previously mentioned, individuals with an SLD can become adept at "hiding" the problem, and so it may not be diagnosed early, or sometimes ever.

How SLDs Are Recognized

Learning difficulties—not necessarily *disorders*—are typically first identified through a screening process, which most elementary school students (should) receive to monitor academic progress. From these screenings, some students may be identified as needing some intervention in one or more areas. For students who do not respond to these various levels of intervention, a more formal identification of an SLD in one or more academic areas may occur. For that to occur, there is a more intensive evaluation process and the involvement of a professional who is qualified to make the official diagnosis, like a school psychologist.

For example, for an individual suspected of dysgraphia, there may be tests for fine motor skills or motor skill planning. Given the involvement of motor skills, occupational or physical therapists may also assist in supporting skill development. When an SLD is identified, parents or guardians, teachers, and other professionals may collaborate to create individualized plans, including individualized education plans (IEPs).

Students who have an SLD receive additional academic support, although they may be at risk for some other social problems. They may deal with feelings of confusion and failure, lack of acceptance among peers, bullying, and absenteeism.

These psychosocial issues associated with SLDs have relevance for sport in a couple of ways. First, upon entering a sport or team, these individuals may bring with them some of the struggles from their academic experiences, including low self-esteem. Sport may be viewed as a way for them to build their self-esteem and also be a release from academic work. In fact, an athlete with an SLD may excel in sports, as they may focus their efforts on what they *can* do (i.e., athleticism) versus what they struggle with (i.e., schoolwork). Therefore, teams can become a safe place for these students, and coaches may be in a unique position to help build confidence and resilience in students, which they can carry back into the classroom and beyond.

While students who are struggling with reading, writing, or mathematics are typically identified in the early school years, these issues are relevant across a span of academic grades and athletic stages and may even never be diagnosed if the individual is adept at hiding the problem. For instance, more than 10% of undergraduate college students may have a learning disability, and student-athletes with an SLD may struggle upon their transition to college. This may be especially true for gifted, collegiate-caliber athletes who were helped to "pass through" their high school academic courses without ideal support. These athletes (and their coaches) may be unfamiliar with the possibilities and processes for accommodations in their college courses. Once again at this level, coaches may be in a unique position to support athletes with SLDs and be part of an effective road map for academic success and athletic eligibility.

Implications for Sport Participation and Performance

The term "unexpected" is often applied to SLDs, meaning that the individuals function typically—and may even outperform their peers—in other areas. Just as students may be labeled as twice exceptional (i.e.having an SLD but being gifted in another academic area), these students may also excel athletically. In this way, when it comes to sport, it may not be evident that a young athlete has an SLD. However, there are many circumstances in practice and competition when a coach would expect their athletes to have basic reading, writing, and mathematical skills. At these times, the challenge(s) the athlete may be experiencing in these domains may be directly, or indirectly, more evident. Directly, when asked to read a playbook, write on a whiteboard, or manage a game clock, these skills may be apparent. More indirectly, athletes may withdraw from these positions and situations. When doing so, athletes are not to be mistaken for being unmotivated, lazy, or defiant. In a report from the National Association for Sport and Physical Education (NASPE, 2012), athletes with SLDs may also demonstrate difficulty in recalling new information, following some directions and routines, and spatial awareness. While an athlete's ability to

perform these may depend upon the severity of the SLD, they are clearly important in sport contexts, including practice and competitions.

Coaching Techniques and Strategies

While coaches are not necessarily able to engage in the targeted instruction aimed at improving literacy, writing, or math skills in the classroom, they can support an athlete's development in many ways. In doing so, they may offer opportunities to practice skills using best practices when working with and teaching athletes sport skills.

Direct instruction may be helpful in teaching sport skills to athletes with SLDs. In direct instruction, steps are broken down sequentially, and athletes are informed of (via dialogue and demonstration) the purpose and outcome of specific steps toward a goal. Additional elements to direct instruction may be segmentation (breaking tasks apart), sequencing, and step-by-step prompts and feedback. Modeling and demonstrating tasks—with verbal cues for the various steps—may also be useful in teaching skills. Athletes may rehearse tasks while also using the verbal cues. In some instances, memory aids or mnemonic devices may also be used to simplify more complex tasks. Once skills are practiced and mastered, athletes with SLDs can perform as well as their peers. These direct strategies may work best when it comes to teaching motor skills used in sport.

As shown in **Table 3.1**, NASPE has offered a variety of ideas and techniques for coaches to consider with athletes with SLDs when it comes to giving directions, demonstrating drills and skills, setting up practice, managing behavior, and creating an environment of social acceptance.

This is not necessarily an exhaustive list of strategies that coaches may employ. There are likely a variety of creative ways in which coaches may communicate to

Table 3.1 Keys to Inclusion of Athletes with Hidden Disabilities

Providing Directions	■ Position yourself close to the athlete to establish eye contact with them while speaking. ■ Ask the athlete to restate your directions to check for understanding. If necessary, repeat directions or provide clarification. ■ Provide directions using multiple modalities. Use visual aids, gestures, and physical prompts along with verbal directions. ■ Chunk information into steps. After each chunk of information, ask the athlete to restate the step to ensure understanding before moving to the next step. ■ Be explicit and consistent with the language and vocabulary you use in explanations and directions. Avoid changing terms or cue words frequently. Clarify terms that appear to confuse the athlete. ■ Use familiar words to deliver clear, concise information about what the athlete should focus on to correct performance. ■ Insist on immediate practice to reinforce the cues.
Demonstrations	■ Explain skills, while providing meaningful demonstrations. ■ Have the athlete use other modalities besides just vision and auditory cues to reinforce the skill. For example, when showing a soccer player how to pass the ball, cue the athlete to attend to the feel where the ball hits their instep, and then use correction cues to reinforce and improve the performance. ■ As an example, ask the athlete to close their eyes while kicking a stationary ball to reinforce this kinesthetic experience. This can help them to develop motor memory for the fundamental motor skills.

Setting Up Practice Activities	■ Focus on establishing an environment of success when choosing activities to include in the practice session. ■ Practice the skill in a whole/part/whole pattern, in which the entire skill is presented first and then broken down into parts, to be combined again as a whole. For example, show the entire corner-kick play, practice the individual movements for each player, and then practice the entire play as a whole again. ■ Chain the skills to be practiced. For example, teach the basketball lay-up by practicing the dribble to the basket, the jump off one foot and the bank shot all separately, and then combined or "chained" together as each skill becomes refined. ■ Offer an entry level and a challenge level for each activity to promote development and inclusion. For example, when practicing striking a baseball, allow some athletes to hit off a tee, some to hit off a toss-up, and others to try to hit off live pitching.
Behavior Management	■ Prevent challenging behaviors before they happen. Provide an appropriate environment that is active and allows athletes to make choices. ■ Implement activities in a way in which athletes will achieve a positive outcome or successful trial a high percentage of the time. ■ Practice in a movement exploration environment where coaches ask all athletes to perform the skill together at their own ability levels (e.g., "dribble as fast as you can, as close to the floor as you can, from one cone to another"). ■ Use proximity control by moving in the immediate area of the athlete who is exhibiting challenging behaviors. ■ Provide positive reinforcement to each athlete who is doing what you asked to encourage continued on-task choices. ■ Redirect inappropriate behavior by requiring a different, more appropriate behavior. For example, if an athlete continues to talk while the coach is talking, ask the athlete to help with the demonstration.
Promoting Social Acceptance	■ Insist that all athletes obey the rules, take turns and practice self-control in becoming more socially aware of others. ■ Allow athletes to function in various leadership roles (e.g., captain, co-captain, stretching leader). ■ Reinforce appropriate and inappropriate social behavior and sportsmanship through team discussions. ■ Deliver opportunities for activities that promote cooperation versus competition, such as focusing on team goals instead of individual goals.

Reproduced from National Association for Sport and Physical Education. (2012). *Coaching athletes with hidden disabilities.* https://www.shapeamerica.org//publications/resources/teachingtools/coachtoolbox/upload/Coaching-Athletes-with-Hidden-Disabilities.pdf their athletes and which may depend on a variety of factors: the individual, type and severity of SLD, and sport and skills being taught. Coaches may also consider reaching out to teachers, parents, and guardians to discuss strategies that may be helpful with the athlete and perhaps transferable to or from school and home environments.

Coaches may be able to facilitate learning with athletes with SLDs. They may find that individuals with SLDs bring characteristics related to resilience, persistence, and mental toughness to sport. They may draw on and emphasize these qualities in practice and competition. Also, coaches may help instill a growth mindset in practice that emphasizes improvement through practice and skill development, which the athlete may translate to academic skills.

Most importantly, coaches must work with the athletes to find solutions to challenges they face. Reading a playbook may be difficult, so can the coach create an audio version or video? If split times confuse an athlete, can splits be color coded instead? If an athlete struggles to distinguish between left and right, can the athlete wear a wristband that serves as an alternative? While each athlete with an SLD will have unique challenges, the coach must be flexible and understanding and work with what knowledge they have to be creative in helping their athlete.

VIGNETTE Part Two

The game was over, the crowd was gone, and Coach Halliwell sat in her office, puzzled. She still didn't get it. She remembered saying 3 to 4 seconds and she remembered Lauren repeating the instructions. Why didn't she wait?

Sighing, she asked Lauren to come into her office. Lauren came in, still excited by the win.

"Hey Coach. Great win," exclaimed Lauren as she sat.

"Yes, it was, wasn't it?" Halliwell responded. "They had a chance to win it at the end though, and if they hadn't traveled, we might not be so happy."

"True, true," said Lauren, realizing how close they had come to losing.

"Lauren, tell me something I've been thinking about. When you took that last shot, what were my instructions about time?"

"2–3 seconds, Coach."

"And how much time was left on the clock when you scored?"

Lauren shifted in her chair. "Uh, well, like 2 seconds."

"But there weren't, Lauren. There were 5 seconds left. I don't understand how you didn't know this."

"Well, I couldn't see the shot clock Coach."

"Couldn't see the shot clock? Come on, Lauren."

"I mean, I looked up but just didn't catch the time."

Halliwell was beginning to get exasperated. She took a breath and thought about what might be going on.

"Okay, okay. I want you to do something for me." Halliwell grabbed her stopwatch and let it run for a few seconds before pausing it. She held it in front of Lauren. "What's the time?"

Lauren squirmed and hesitated. "Uh, 4.6 seconds, Coach."

"No Lauren. It's 6.3. What is it you're seeing?"

"I can't see anything! It's just like a blur to me. Like the numbers keep moving and won't stay still! The same thing happens in math class and I hate it. Does this mean I can't play?" Lauren was close to tears.

"No, of course it doesn't, Lauren." Halliwell got up and came around her desk. "It's okay. This is a challenge, but we'll work together and figure out how the school and I can help you succeed."

Additional Resources

- Council for Exceptional Children: https://www.cec.sped.org/
- Decoding Dyslexia: http://www.decodingdyslexia.net/dd-states.html
- International Dyslexia Association: https://dyslexiaida.org/
- Learning Disabilities Association of America: https://ldaamerica.org/
- National Center on Improving Literacy: https://improvingliteracy.org/
- Understood: https://www.understood.org/

Summary

- SLDs relate to a range of difficulties in learning and application of academic skills. Given the focus on difficulties with academic skills, SLDs tend to be in areas typically found in school, including reading, writing, and mathematics.
    - Dyslexia (reading)
    - Dysgraphia (writing)
    - Dyscalculia (numerical information and mathematics)
- SLDs are "unexpected" in that the individuals function and perform typically—and may even outperform their peers—in other areas. These students may excel athletically.
- In sport, it may not be evident that a young athlete has an SLD. However, there are many circumstances in practice and competition when a coach can envision requiring the basic reading, writing, and mathematical skills of their athletes.
- There exist a variety of ideas and techniques for coaches to consider with athletes with SLDs when it comes to:
    - Giving directions
    - Demonstrating drills and skills
    - Setting up practice
    - Managing behavior
    - Creating an environment of social acceptance
- Coaches may find that individuals with SLDs bring characteristics related to resilience, persistence, and mental toughness to sport. They may draw on and emphasize these qualities in practice and competition.

Questions for Consideration

1. What are the similarities between dyslexia, dysgraphia, and dyscalculia?
2. What are the differences between dyslexia, dysgraphia, and dyscalculia?
3. What does "2e" stand for and what are the implications?
4. Give three examples not included in the book showing how SLDs might manifest themselves in a sporting situation. Consider your own sport.
5. What do you think is the most important coaching technique and strategy when considering SLDs? Why?

References

American Psychiatric Association. (2013). Specific Learning Disorder. In *Diagnostic and statistical manual of mental disorders* (5th ed.).

Braun, R., & Braun, B. (2015). Managing the challenges of hidden disabilities in youth sport: A look at SLD, ADHD, and ASD through the sport psychology lens. *Journal of Sport Psychology in Action*, 6(1), 28–43.

Forster-Scott, L. (2019). At-risk athletes. In J. Taylor (Ed.), *Comprehensive Applied Sport Psychology* (pp. 227–232). Routledge.

Gersten, R. (1996). Literacy instruction for language-minority students: The transition years. *The Elementary School Journal*, *96*(3), 227–244.

Lyon, G. R., Shaywitz, S. E., & Shaywitz, B. A. (2003). A definition of dyslexia. *Annals of Dyslexia*, *53*(1), 1–14. https://www.jstor.org/stable/23764731

Muter, V., & Snowling, M. J. (2009). Children at familial risk of dyslexia: Practical implications from an at-risk study. *Child and Adolescent Mental Health*, *14*(1), 37–41.

National Association for Sport and Physical Education. (2012). *Coaching athletes with hidden disabilitiess*. Retrieved from https://www.shapeamerica.org//publications/resources/teachingtools/coachtoolbox/upload/Coaching-Athletes-with-Hidden-Disabilities.pdf

Peterson, R. L., & Pennington, B. F. (2015). Developmental dyslexia. *Annual Review of Clinical Psychology*, *11*, 283–307.

Snowling, M. J. (2012). Changing concepts of dyslexia: Nature, treatment and comorbidity. *Journal of Child Psychology and Psychiatry*, *53*(9), e1–e3. https://doi.org/10.1111/j.1469-7610.2009.02197.x

Undheim, A. M. (2003). Dyslexia and psychosocial factors. A follow-up study of young Norwegian adults with a history of dyslexia in childhood. *Nordic Journal of Psychiatry*, *57*(3), 221–226.

CHAPTER 4

Autism Spectrum Disorder

VIGNETTE Part One

"That's it!" exclaimed Jared as he slumped onto the bench next to his head coach and dropped his racquet on the floor. "I can't take it, Coach! I just can't take it anymore. I can't play with him. It's totally messing up my game, and now even when I play singles."

This past weekend, Jared and his partner, Isaac, had lost another close tennis match against their college rivals. The loss was still stinging two days later when head coach Kenyon Samuel asked them to practice together. Practice hadn't gone well, and Jared had had enough.

"Talk to me," Coach Samuel said, trying to calm down the situation.

"It's crazy. He's driving me nuts! He barely talks to me at all on the court. If he hits a good shot, I tell him "good shot" but when I hit one he does nothing. The louder I get the more he seems to shut down. And he's got this weird fidget while I'm serving and it's so distracting. He doesn't talk strategy during the game so I'm trying to figure it out myself. Sometimes, it's like he's off in a different world. We often play well once the points start, but there's no chemistry outside of that. Honestly Coach, I don't care how good he is, and although we win more than we lose, I just don't like him. He doesn't joke around, he doesn't hang out with the rest of the team, and he's unsocial, like he's better than us."

Coach Samuel nodded, listening without trying to judge one player in front of another. "Okay, I've seen some of this too, but let's not be too quick to judge. He's a freshman and is still learning."

"That's not an excuse," Jared retorted. "I've played with other freshmen before and never had this trouble. This is an Isaac problem."

"Alright, Jared. I know you're frustrated, but I want to learn more. I get where you're coming from, but I need to talk with Isaac as well. Don't give up on him yet."

Coach Samuel watched as Jared headed for the showers. Usually, his team had excellent chemistry, but he'd struggled to figure out Isaac. He was an extremely talented athlete, but after trying a variety of doubles pairings, the response always seemed to be the same; no one felt comfortable playing with him. What was going on?

Forms, Definitions, and Prevalence

Autism spectrum disorder (ASD), often shortened to *autism*, is related to a range of social and behavioral symptoms, which impact how the individual perceives, interacts, and communicates with others. It can also involve limited and repetitive behavioral patterns, shown through repetitive motor movement, strict adherence to routines, fixation on certain topics or interests, or different reactions to sensations (American Psychiatric Association, 2013).

The term "spectrum" is used because there is such a range of social and behavioral factors as well as severities. These can range from individuals requiring some support under certain circumstances to requiring very substantial support. The autism spectrum captures disorders that were previously (before 2013) diagnosed separately, including Asperger's disorder, Rett's disorder, and childhood disintegrative disorder. For ASD, the support(s) needed can depend on the environment or current situation and can also change over time. The considerations of severity and environment may impact how "hidden" ASD may actually be to others, including coaches in sport environments. ASD does not necessarily impact athletic capabilities, although any negative social and motor factors could impact sport participation and performance in various ways. According to the National Autism Association, approximately 1 in 54 children (or almost 2%) have ASD, and boys are more likely to have it than girls.

How ASD Is Recognized

ASD is brain-based; certain regions of the brain related to social behaviors, communication, and other cognitive functioning develop atypically. ASD usually begins to appear in one or more ways very early in childhood, before the age of 3. One of

the ways ASD can be recognized early is through language development, including a delay in first words. Motor deficits may also show themselves early on in terms of abnormal walking, running gait, or appearance of clumsiness. In other cases, there may be apparent slowing or even freezing of motor behavior in the middle of an action sequence.

These linguistic, social, and motor difficulties can negatively impact learning in school environments. At home, the child may follow a routine that helps with their sleep, diet, and health care (e.g., doctor's visits, dental appointments, haircuts). Individuals with ASD may experience difficulties in learning and social interactions throughout life, although they can develop compensatory strategies and skills that help them. In most cases, individuals with ASD demonstrate improvement in social areas into late childhood and adolescence. They may begin to form healthy friendships and mutually beneficial social relationships. However, individuals with ASD may be more likely to be bullied and more vulnerable to experience symptoms of anxiety and depression.

Implications for Sport Participation and Performance

The associated challenges with social connections and communication can impact learning with instructors and peers for individuals with ASD. This may extend to sport situations with coaches and teammates learning new skills and strategies through drills. It may also extend to the ability to develop relationships with coaches and teammates, even after extensive time spent together. In addition, the need to maintain a strict adherence to routines and the possibility of becoming overstimulated may impact how easily athletes with ASD are able to transition into sport, new seasons, coaches, or teammates. Again, the severity of the symptoms and situation may dictate if these can be observed by the coach, in what area(s), and to what degree.

Coaching Techniques and Strategies

Braun and Braun (2015) offered a useful review of educational strategies, which may be considered and adopted for use in sport situations for athletes with ASD. They suggest targeting three core areas, which broadly relate to the social, behavioral, and communicative or linguistic areas that define ASD:

- Strategies are developed with consideration of overstimulation.
- Usage of appropriate level of language.
- Development of social skills and sensitivity to special interests and skills.

For strategies related to sensory overstimulation, coaches must think about the practice environment. Understandably, this may be challenging, as many sport contexts have many people and activities with inherent movement and noise. There are any number of stimulating experiences during sport, including tactile (physical interaction with people and objects), visual (observation of drills, ball movement), and audible (coaches' instructions and feedback, teammates' communication). Coaches should work with athletes, parents and guardians and others

© Patrik Giardino/Stone/Getty Images.

to identify sensations, intensities, or events that seem to spark a negative response in any given athlete.

For example, an athlete with ASD may appear particularly distressed during certain drills that require prolonged physical contact with others. Another athlete with ASD may respond negatively to sharp audible stimuli such as whistles, horns, or starting pistols. Coaches who are typically loud or yell during practices and games may realize that athletes with ASD react negatively to the intensity of the communication. Coaches must understand these "triggers," which may invoke overstimulation, and attempt to refrain from yelling at players in general, unless it is about something positive.

Additionally, coaches may always provide and communicate a "plan of escape" for these athletes. This plan could include a discrete word or gesture, which the athlete can communicate to the coach to let them know they are overstimulated. Then, there could be an agreed-upon location, presumably with less stimulation, or a set of tasks that the athlete could transition to for a period of time. For example, some athletes may find solitary walking or running to be calming, and there may be room to fill in with this activity during certain times. Athletes with ASD may find the company of select individuals (like coaches) on such activities to be helpful, if it's possible.

When considering communication, coaches should consider language as it occurs linguistically (through spoken words) and physically (through body language and gestures). Athletes with ASD may process and perceive all forms of communication differently. For instance, individuals with ASD may take spoken words quite literally, so coaches may consider how often they use metaphors, sarcasm, or other nonliteral forms of speech in their communication with the team or with

specific individuals. In addition, individuals with ASD may also not pick up on social cues, including body language. Together, simple and straightforward communication that is presented calmly and succinctly to these athletes may work best. Coaches should consider using the same terms consistently to express their ideas, and these may be presented at the relevant, predictable intervals or places throughout practice and competitions (warm-ups, drills, feedback, etc.). If there are situations in which teammates are broken into smaller groups, coaches may consider carefully with which teammate(s) an athlete with ASD is paired. A teammate (or more) who is patient and communicates clearly may work best in such group activities.

When trying to teach new skills, coaches may consider *video modeling*, which has been demonstrated to be effective in educational settings with children with ASD (Wong et al., 2015). Judge and Morgan (2020) described the four core types of video modeling and how they can be applied to sports situations:

- Basic modeling—the athlete can view others performing a skill and then imitate.
- Self-modeling—athletes can watch themselves performing a skill *successfully.*
- Point-of-view modeling—video from a first-person perspective. This form of modeling demonstrates what it looked like for the athlete themselves going through the motor movements.
- Video prompting—more complex skills are broken down with pauses in between segments. Athletes progress with the successful completion of each stage.

Coaches may also make use of special interests and skills of athletes with ASD and explore ways in which these athletes may be the team "expert" in certain areas. For instance, some athletes may like to delve deeply into history, information, and numbers. These athletes may benefit from being able to assist with or manage team stats and information. A special interest in technology may work well if the athlete can help manage files and team communication, create or manage practice or game videos, or even explore new technology that they think may help the coach or team. For the coach, it will be helpful to get to know their athlete(s)' special interests, and if new special interests in sport contexts are emerging.

Athletes with a tendency to fixate attentionally on certain tasks or movements may be prompted to do so with various skills in sport. In some ways, this may be a competitive advantage for athletes with ASD in mastering new or difficult skills. For some athletes with ASD, the routines inherent in sport (set-up, warm-ups, preperformance routines) may become particularly rigid. Inevitably, these routines will be disrupted for a variety of reasons, both anticipated (new equipment, new drills) and unanticipated (weather, delays). When they are anticipated, coaches may communicate in advance of the "change" date to the athletes, helping them to become prepared. Coaches may also consider slowly introducing the new material, perhaps through brief exposure to new equipment or drills or observation of new activities.

VIGNETTE Part Two

Coach Samuel heard a knock on his office door and looked up. It was Jared.

"Hi, Jared. Thanks for coming in."

"Sure, Coach. What's up?"

"Have a seat. Well, you talked to me the other day about your struggles with Isaac, and I've talked with Isaac and wanted to share a little of what he said to me with you. I asked his permission, but he also asked me to only share this with you, as it's a bit sensitive for him."

"Uh, okay." Jared began to look uncomfortable, but Coach Samuel continued.

"I've obviously noticed the same things as you about Isaac since he joined our program. I talked to the coaching staff about it as well, and so I talked to him about it. The reason I asked you in is because several years ago he was diagnosed with a form of autism. It affects the way he interacts with people and he struggles to socialize with others. Sometimes, he doesn't understand sarcasm, or he takes things literally. This is why you think he's standoffish and not really a team player. He and his family didn't share this with us during recruiting because they were worried it would affect his chances of a scholarship."

Jared nodded, beginning to understand, and Coach Samuel took Jared through the specific challenges Isaac faced on a daily basis.

"I asked Isaac to help me come up with a list of things that he struggles with, and then we worked on ideas that might help him in those situations." Coach Samuel grabbed the list from his desk and handed it to Jared. "Obviously, this is a work in progress, but as his doubles partner, I wanted you to know before I talked to the others. This is hard for Isaac to talk about, and I hope you'll be more understanding. I think we can all work together to make him more comfortable, and I've no doubt the more comfortable he becomes, the less likely he will be to do and say some of the things we've seen."

"Thanks Coach. Uh, yeah, this is something I didn't see coming, but now that I see it, it makes sense. I guess I need to talk to him and apologize. Now that I know, I think we can try to make it work."

Additional Resources

- Autism Speaks: https://www.autismspeaks.org/resource-guide
- Center for Disease Control and Prevention: https://www.cdc.gov/ncbddd/autism/facts.html
- National Autism Association: https://nationalautismassociation.org/
- US Department of Education/Office of Special Education Programs: https://sites.ed.gov/idea/osep-fast-facts-children-with-autism-20/

Summary

- ASD is related to a range of social and behavioral symptoms that impact how the individual perceives, interacts, and communicates with others. It can also involve a rigid or repetitive behavioral routine.
- Approximately 2% of children have ASD, and boys are more likely than girls to have it.
- Individuals with ASD may experience difficulties in learning and social interactions throughout life, although they can develop compensatory strategies and skills that help them.
- The challenges with social connections and communication can impact learning and may extend to sport situations with coaches and teammates learning new skills and strategies through drills. It may also extend to the ability to develop relationships with coaches and teammates.
- Some core educational approaches may be helpful for coaches to employ with athletes with ASD, including:
  1. Strategies that are developed with consideration of overstimulation
  2. Usage of appropriate level of language
  3. Development of social skills and sensitivity to special interests and skills
- Coaches may also embrace the special interests and skills of athletes with ASD. Coaches may explore ways in which these athletes may be the team "expert" in certain areas.
- Athletes with a tendency to fixate attentionally on certain tasks or movements may be prompted to do so with various skills in sport.

Questions for Consideration

1. What does the term "spectrum" refer to? Give some examples.
2. A child with ASD is more likely to be _________ and more vulnerable to experience _____________ of ____________ and ________________.
3. Provide three coaching techniques and strategies to help an athlete with ASD.
4. What is the purpose of a "plan of escape?"
5. Explain the four types of modeling and how they are important for someone with ASD.

References

American Psychiatric Association. (2013). Autism Spectrum Disorder. In *Diagnostic and statistical manual of mental disorders* (5th ed.).

Braun, R., & Braun, B. (2015). Managing the challenges of hidden disabilities in youth sport: A look at SLD, ADHD, and ASD through the sport psychology lens. *Journal of Sport Psychology in Action*, 6(1), 28–43.

Judge, J. P., & Morgan, K. N. (2020). Video modeling: Strategies to support physical activity in children with Autism Spectrum Disorder. *Palaestra*, *34*(2), 37–42.

Wong, C., Odom, S. L., Hume, K. A., Cox, A. W., Fettig, A., Kucharczyk, S., Brock, M. E., Plavnick, J. B., Fleury, V. P., & Schultz, T. R. (2015). Evidence-based practices for children, youth, and young adults with autism spectrum disorder: A comprehensive review. *Journal of Autism and Developmental Disorders*, *45*(7), 1951–1966.

CHAPTER 5

Attention-Deficit/ Hyperactivity Disorder (ADHD)

VIGNETTE Part One

"Coach, he's doing it again!"

Coach Sally Alum looked up at her volunteer assistant, who pointed to the other side of the field. There, running toward the trees and the end of the practice field was Dexter, intent on something other than soccer.

"Not again," groaned Alum inwardly as she stopped her drill with her group and took off after him. "I'm a parent of a 7-year-old on this team, only a coach because no one stepped up, and totally didn't sign up for this!"

Dexter was close to disappearing into the trees, and she wasn't sure she was going to catch him, but just before he got there, he stopped abruptly, knelt down, and started studying the ground. Alum breathed a sigh of relief as she caught up with him and slowed down. She stood above him as he studied the ground intently, almost like she wasn't there.

"Hey Dexter, whatcha doing?"

"Looking at bugs," responded Dexter.

"I see. Well, we're practicing soccer and you just ran off. You can't just do that, okay? We're here to practice soccer."

"Yeah, but the bugs are cool!"

"I know, but maybe after practice you can look for bugs with your parents. Right now, we need to get back to the group, okay?"

"But these bugs are cool! This one has an exoskeleton."

"Yes, I know. But later." Dexter didn't seem willing to move. Coach Sally sighed, not sure what to do. This wasn't the first time something like this had happened with Dexter, and she wasn't sure it would be the last. This was a volunteer soccer program in the community, and the only reason she was there was because all of the other parents were "too busy" to help. Fortunately, another mom had stepped up to help as her assistant, and while Alum had played soccer in college, she sure wasn't equipped to handle this kind of situation. A conversation with Dexter's parents had to happen, but what to say and how to help?

Forms, Definitions, and Prevalence

Attention-deficit/hyperactivity disorder (ADHD) is reflected in a persistent pattern of inattention and/or hyperactivity (or impulsivity), which can interfere with daily functioning and impair development, including in learning and social contexts. Someone with ADHD may predominantly demonstrate inattention, hyperactivity/impulsivity, or both. The term "ADD"—referring to attention deficit disorder—is sometimes used to refer to ADHD where the inattention symptoms are most evident (American Psychiatric Association, 2013).

Like other neurodevelopmental disorders, there is a brain basis for ADHD. The group of skills or symptoms related to ADHD, such as attention, planning, and inhibition, may be referred to as *executive functioning*. For individuals with ADHD, the areas of the brain linked with executive functioning may take longer to develop or some neurological pathways may be less efficient.

Like other neurodevelopmental disorders (e.g., autism spectrum), severity can range from mild (cases where few, if any, symptoms are severe enough to impair functioning in more than minor ways) to severe (many symptoms are present and are severe enough to make a large, negative impact on functioning and development). Once again, the level of severity may determine how observable or hidden ADHD would be to coaches and fellow athletes. While estimates vary, according to the Centers for Disease Control and Prevention (CDC), approximately 10% of children between the ages of 4 and 17 have been diagnosed with ADHD, more commonly in males than females. In females, it is more common for inattention to be more apparent.

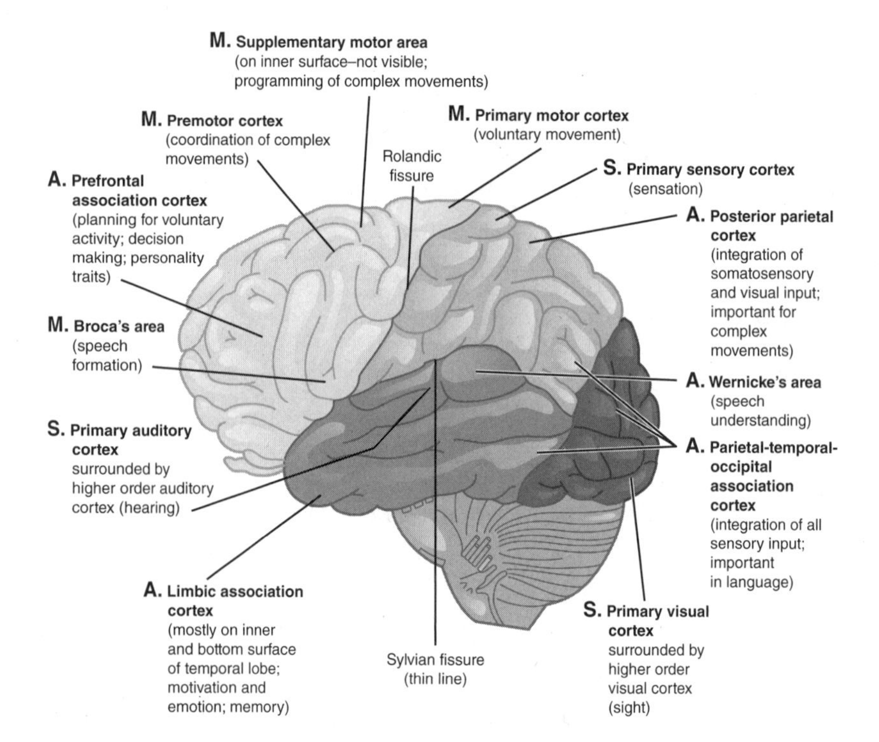

The *inattention* in ADHD may be observed in persistent wandering (off tasks), difficulty maintaining concentration or focus on tasks, a general lack of persistence in tasks, and apparent disorganization. In the context of ADHD, inattention may show itself in careless mistakes and lack of attention to detail, not seeming to pay attention when spoken to, not following through on instructions, avoidance of tasks that require sustained effort or focus, easily distractible, and seemingly forgetful. While inattention may be broadly evident, some individuals with ADHD may also demonstrate a hyper-focus on tasks they find particularly interesting.

The *hyperactivity* evident in some cases of ADHD refers to excessive motor activity when it is not otherwise appropriate or necessary, such as running, or excessive fidgeting or talking. Hyperactive individuals may also seem restless to others. The *impulsivity* symptoms may include hurried, spontaneous action(s) seemingly without forethought and sometimes have a higher potential for harm to oneself. Someone with ADHD who also displays hyperactive/impulsive behaviors may often leave assigned spaces (seats, spots in line), may run or climb in appropriate situations, talk excessively or out of turn, and may seem to interrupt others or intrude on others in terms of conversations, activities, etc. (American Psychiatric Association, 2013).

While some degree of inattention, hyperactivity, and impulsivity is common in all children, for children with ADHD, the symptoms can be persistent, severe, and interfere with functioning at home, school, athletics, and other contexts. Communication among caregivers and coaches can be helpful for coaches to help prepare for the athlete.

How ADHD Is Recognized

The symptoms and patterns associated with ADHD begin in childhood. Excessive motor activity may be the first observable symptom, although before the age of 4 or 5 this may be difficult to differentiate between normal, but high rates of activity. During early elementary school, when there is increased need to regulate behaviors, such as pay attention to class rules or assignment instructions, stand in line or wait for a turn, and remain in one's seat, is when symptoms of ADHD may become more apparent to caregivers and educators. Over time and into adolescence, hyperactivity may diminish in the form of running, jumping, and climbing and become more restricted to fidgeting and a sense of being jittery or restless (Turnbull et al, 2006).

As these symptoms become more observable in academic situations, they may also interfere with social and academic skill development. The behaviors associated with inattention (wandering, lack of focus), hyperactivity (excessive talking, restlessness, not taking turns) and impulsivity (spontaneous or risky behaviors, interruptions) may cause some educators to view athletes with ADHD as problematic, or troublemakers. This is not true—ADHD is not a matter of will power or laziness.

Implications for Sport Participation and Performance

In sport contexts, with coaches needing athletes to pay attention (e.g., rules, movement and skill demonstrations, drills, feedback, etc.), an athlete with ADHD (with symptoms of inattention) could be impacted in numerous ways. In addition, hyperactive and impulsive behaviors could present an array of challenges in the sport environment. It has been estimated that about half of individuals with ADHD have motor difficulties and perhaps especially fine motor movements. These difficulties may translate into challenges performing the physical movements and tasks inherent in sport.

Interestingly, some research has shown that the physical activity in sport can help reduce ADHD symptoms. One study demonstrated that higher levels of physical activity were associated with better executive functioning (e.g., memory, inhibition), particularly with planning tasks (Gapin & Etnier, 2010). In another study, researchers found that a variety of motor skills (e.g., throwing a ball for distance or accuracy, standing long jump, bead stringing, ball striking) could improve cognitive performance, particular inhibition, or the ability to resist, control, or stop behaviors (Hung et al., 2013). These findings don't imply that these skills or drills are well suited specifically to help athletes with ADHD, but indicate that physical activity, movement, and motor skill development may in and of themselves be beneficial for athletes with ADHD.

Coaching Techniques and Strategies

With some basic strategies aimed at focusing attention, reducing complexity of instructions and tasks, and minimizing cognitive load, greater success can be achieved with coaching athletes with ADHD. For example, to address tendencies of inattention, the coach may benefit from simplifying instructions by "chunking" information into more manageable amounts. This may be particularly useful if drills, directions, or movement are complex in nature. One chunking method is usage of *mnemonic devices*, which help simplify information for better memory retrieval. Another helpful method may be usage of visual or auditory aids, such as signs, images, or cue cards. These could be used by coaches or teammates (perhaps from the sideline) to help refocus attention on relevant tasks.

Other considerations for coaches when it comes to inattentiveness of athletes:

- During instructional times, the athlete may be in quiet areas and/or near good role models.
- Shorten instructional work periods to meet attention span of athletes. Use a timer if helpful and offer brief breaks between work periods.
- Offer clear, concise directions on techniques and skills being learned.
- Set up a cue or signal with the athlete to discretely communicate for them to stay on task.
- Work with athlete to set short-term, daily goals.

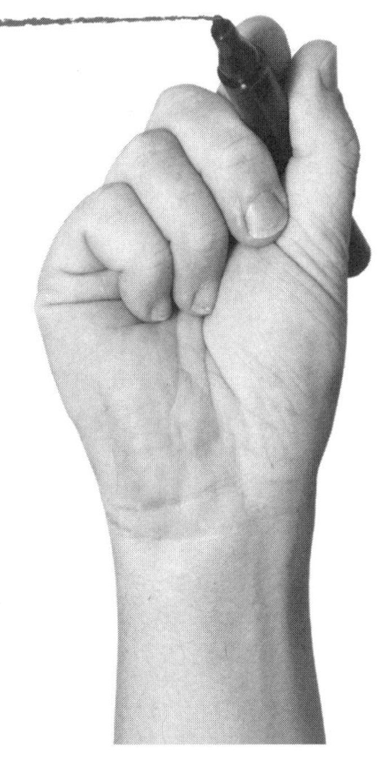

© Jones & Bartlett Learning.

Coaches and athletes could have "goals of the day" in which they mutually agree upon a manageable number of items on which they can focus. Goal setting, while an important fundamental element of sport for all athletes, may be particularly helpful for coaches to emphasize with athletes with ADHD. Goals should be *specific, measurable, achievable, realistic, timely* (SMART). Goals should be SMART so athletes and coaches can more easily (self) monitor goal progress and attainment. For athletes who have motoric difficulties associated with ADHD, coaches may offer extra time or reps to complete drills or tasks successfully (Braun & Braun, 2015).

For athletes with impulsive tendencies, the coach may consider or benefit from:

- Initially ignoring what may seem like minor inappropriate behavior from an athlete.
- Monitoring "transitional" times, such as those periods between drills, or before and after practice and games.
- Being clear with all athletes about what is expected in terms of behavior and conduct in sport environments.
- Increasing immediacy of rewards and reinforcements for positive behaviors. Visibly recognize positive efforts and behaviors from all athletes.

VIGNETTE Part Two

Coach Sally Alum approached Dexter's dad after practice. She knew it wouldn't be a fun conversation, but it had to occur.

"Hi Trevor, can I have a quick word?"

"Sure. What's up?" Trevor asked.

"Well, we've had a couple of situations with Dexter during practice that have concerned us. He's not doing anything to others, and he's a great kid, but he gets distracted quite easily. Normally, this wouldn't bother me, but a couple of times, he's wandered off toward the trees or will just stop doing what we're all doing and ignore everyone and everything. It's like he gets fixated on something other than what we're doing. I know this program is just to have fun and get some exercise, but I'm a little concerned for his safety too. Today, he almost ran into the trees before we could catch him." Sally paused, but before she could continue, Trevor responded.

"Yeah, I'm sorry about that, and I'm sorry my wife didn't tell you. I thought she had."

"Tell me what?"

"Well, he's been diagnosed with a mild form of ADHD so he can sometimes struggle to pay attention and stay focused on tasks."

Now it began to make sense to Sally. "Ah. I see. That definitely explains a lot."

"Yeah, I'm sorry. We should have told you in advance."

"Well, now that I do know, perhaps you could help me. It would really help if you could put together a list of things related to soccer that Dexter can do well, focus on, and things that he struggles with. Then, could you come up with strategies that we can use to help him be successful? I think that would help both he and us."

"Yeah, of course. We can do that."

"Thanks!" Sally breathed an internal sigh of relief. It still wasn't going to be easy, but at least she'd have something to work with.

Additional Resources

- Center for Disease Control and Prevention: https://www.cdc.gov/ncbddd/adhd/facts.html
- Children and Adults with Attention-Deficit/Hyperactivity Disorder (CHADD): https://chadd.org/
- Understood: https://www.understood.org/en/learning-thinking-differences/child-learning-disabilities/add-adhd/what-is-adhd

Summary

- ADHD is reflected in a persistent pattern of inattention and/or hyperactivity (or impulsivity), which can interfere with daily functioning and impair development, including in learning and social contexts as well as sport.
- Approximately 10% of children between the ages of 4 and 17 have been diagnosed with ADHD; it is more common in males.
- The symptoms and patterns associated with ADHD begin in childhood. In cases where hyperactivity is present, excessive motor activity may be the first observable symptoms.
- Using basic strategies aimed at focusing attention, reducing complexity of instructions and tasks, and also minimizing cognitive load, greater success can be achieved in coaching athletes with ADHD.

Questions for Consideration

1. What is the prevalence of ADHD? Do you think it is becoming more or less prevalent? What evidence do you have for this opinion?
2. Are males or females more likely to have ADHD?
3. The research of Gapin & Etnier (2010) and Hung et al. (2013) suggest some important findings. What are they?
4. If an athlete seems to be inattentive, what can you do as a coach to help?
5. If an athlete tends to be impulsive, what can you do as a coach to help?

References

American Psychiatric Association. (2013). Attention-Deficit/Hyperactivity Disorder. In *Diagnostic and statistical manual of mental disorders* (5th ed.).

Braun, R., & Braun, B. (2015). Managing the challenges of hidden disabilities in youth sport: A look at SLD, ADHD, and ASD through the sport psychology lens. *Journal of Sport Psychology in Action*, 6(1), 28–43.

Centers for Disease Control and Prevention. (2020). *ADHD throughout the years*. https://www.cdc.gov/ncbddd/adhd/timeline.html

Gapin, J., & Etnier, J. L. (2010). The relationship between physical activity and executive function performance in children with attention-deficit hyperactivity disorder. *Journal of Sport and Exercise Psychology*, 32(6), 753–763.

Hung, C. L., Chang, Y. K., Chan, Y. S., Shih, C. H., Huang, C. J., & Hung, T. M. (2013). Motor ability and inhibitory processes in children with ADHD: A neuroelectric study. *Journal of Sport and Exercise Psychology*, 35(3), 322–328.

Turnbull, A., Turnbull, R., Wehmeyer, M. L., & Shogren, K. A. (2006). *Exceptional lives* (9th ed.). Pearson.

PART 3

Sensory Conditions and Communication

CHAPTER 6

Sensory Processing Disorder

VIGNETTE Part One

Coach Pat Louden looked to the bench for her next hitter. There sat Nika, away from the others, oblivious to what was going on. Pat sighed, wishing it was someone else at bat. Nika wasn't a bad player, but with the game on the line, she needed her best.

"Nika," shouted Pat. Nika looked up startled. "You're up on deck, Nika. We need a good hit and a chance to run it home. We need two runs so take what you can get." The deer-in-the-headlights look from Nika didn't inspire Pat, but Nika nodded, stood up, and skirted around the mess of a long 7-inning battle uncomfortably, before carefully tiptoeing out of the dugout.

While Pat didn't feel too optimistic, Nika surprised even her when she blasted a ball down the left field line. There were screams from the dugout, and Nika stuttered out off the plate toward first base. Sensing an opportunity, her first base coach waved her through, so Nika kept running. It would be tight into second, but with a solid slide under the glove, Nika would make it. But... Nika didn't slide. Instead, her run slowed as she approached the base. Pat watched in disbelief as the second base opponent caught the ball, turned, and touched her glove to Nika's approaching knee. Nika almost flinched at the touch. Out, signaled the umpire emphatically. Pat couldn't believe it. Third out, lights out, game over.

Forms, Definitions, and Prevalence

Sensory processing disorder (SPD), sometimes also referred to as sensory integration dysfunction, is the inability to process information received through one or more of the senses. The dysfunction occurs in the central nervous system, including the brain, which is unable to efficiently process, organize, and analyze (i.e., integrate) sensory messages (**Figure 6.1**). With such difficulties processing incoming stimuli, there are also challenges in the ways in which the individual with SPD responds with efficiency or accuracy to environmental demands. Those with SPD may generally appear to react in disorganized ways, perhaps being

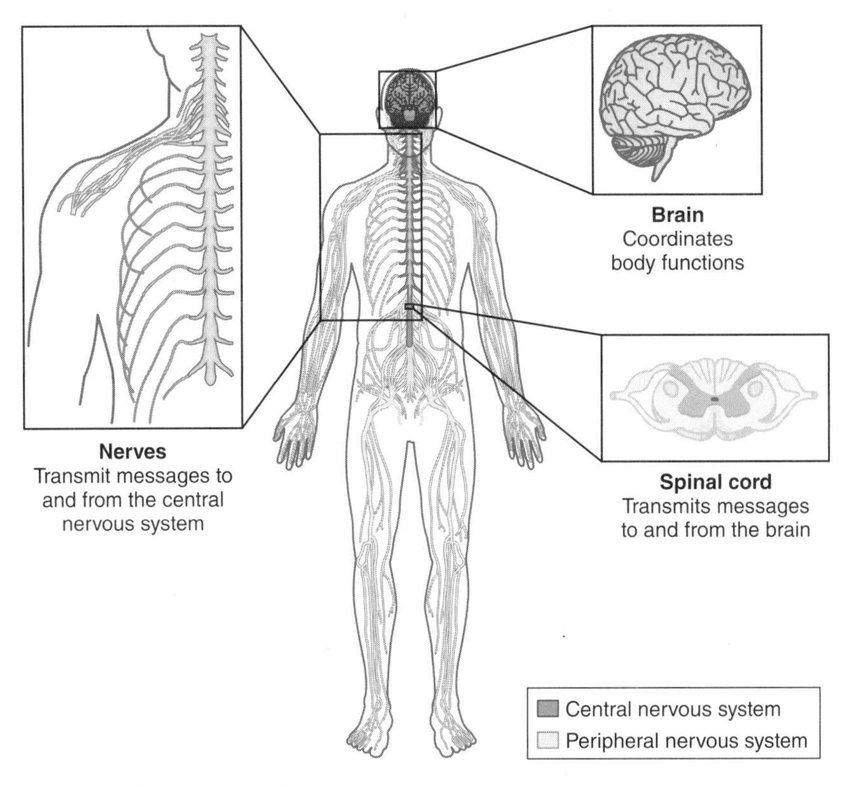

Figure 6.1 The central nervous system.

"out-of-sync" with the environment. One in 20 individuals (5%) or more may be impacted by SPD (Kranowitz & Archer, 1998; Miller et al., 2014).

The symptoms of SPD, like other conditions, exist on a spectrum. Individuals with SPD may have difficulty with one, two, or multiple senses. In addition, they may be highly over- or under-responsive to stimuli. Generally, the *over-responsive* individual may seek or need less stimulation, while the under-responsive may seek out more. For instance, in terms of tactile or touch sensations, the over-responsive individual with SPD may actively avoid touching—or being touched by—people or objects. They may also avoid getting dirty or be averse to certain textures of clothing or food. These same individuals may be averse to moving spontaneously, and appear "earthbound" as they avoid running, climbing, jumping, swinging, or otherwise being off balance

On the other hand, someone *under-responsive* may seem unresponsive to or unaware of pain or touch. They may play with objects seemingly without purpose, or bump into objects or people. They may also be prone to constant movement, such as running or spinning. However, one of the core ways to recognize SPD may be the atypical responses to tactile sensations, including being touched or moved. Interestingly, SPD is not a stand-alone medical diagnosis, although medical professionals and occupational therapists may still be led to SPD to clarify a child's sensory challenges or behavioral problems. While SPD is not an SLD, it can lead to learning disabilities when it negatively impacts academic learning (Kranowitz & Archer, 1998; Miller et al., 2014).

According to the STAR Institute, SPD symptoms may be comorbid (or simultaneously present) with some other conditions covered in this book. For instance, the under-responsiveness or over-responsiveness can often be observed in ASD, leading the two to be mistaken for one another from time to time. STAR also reports that while most (75%) children with ASD have significant symptoms of SPD, the reverse is not true. Most children with SPD do *not* have ASD. Similarly, SPD and ADHD can be mistaken for one another, particularly when children with an under-responsive form of SPD consistently and actively seek out new sensations. Given the overlap in some symptomology, assessment from a qualified medical professional is important.

The STAR Institute (website offered in resources at the end of this chapter) also has many resources to help understand sensory processing difficulties. For instance, they offer an SPD Treatment Directory to help locate qualified professionals. Another set of resources is age-appropriate "checklists," which can help identify sensory issues that may exist outside of a typical range. The checklists are not screening or identification tools but can help facilitate understanding and dialogue with doctors.

How SPD Is Recognized

Those with SPD may start out being described as fussy babies and may resist change as evident with sensory meltdowns. As they age, they may exhibit anxiousness with new situations or stimuli. With difficulties processing and responding to the new information with SPD, adaptive (e.g., responding to new information or situations), academic (e.g., school tasks), and motor (e.g., physical movements and athletic skills) learning in a variety of contexts can be negatively impacted.

Implications for Sport Participation and Performance

Numerous implications for play and sport may be drawn from SPD symptoms. Difficulties with processing environmental information and learning can impact motor development and learning, processing of feedback, and attention and concentration, to name a few. Moreover, with SPD, more than just the five more commonly known senses (i.e., touch, taste, smell, sight, and hearing) can be impacted. For instance, *interoception* is sense related to how one feels in their own bodies. In addition, *proprioception* (bodily awareness in relation to other people and objects in the environment) and *spatial orientation* can also be impacted. Balance, as well as internal and external bodily awareness has far-reaching consequences for sport. Complex movements such as those in gymnastics may be examples where these sensory systems are used heavily, although they are also necessary in simpler movements (e.g., batting stance, running to a ball in the field of play, jumping to rebound a ball). The STAR Institute website has a helpful section on the eight sensory systems, with descriptions and examples.

Coaching Techniques and Strategies

Sensory processing problems are not a result of lack of discipline or mental toughness, and athletes with SPD would not necessarily respond well to a rigid, disciplinarian approach. It is important to note that school and sport can be difficult for individuals with SPD. For instance, there is pressure to conform and perform, there can be abrupt transitions from one subject or task to the next, stimuli can be overwhelming at times (e.g., lights, noises, odors), and at other times, not stimulating enough (e.g., long stretches of sitting). With some forethought and adaptability, coaches can make the team and practice environments more welcoming for athletes with SPD. Some of the approaches that coaches can take mirror those teachers may take in the classroom. Relevant considerations may focus on:

- Reducing sensory overload (where applicable)
- Managing practice environments
- Helping the athletes become more organized
- Adapting one's own behavior

In terms of reducing sensory overload, coaches may need to observe the sensations(s) that appear to be most distracting. For instance, for those with sensitivity to tactile (touch) sensations, consider giving the athlete as much space as possible (e.g., during warm-ups, team talks, line drills, etc.) to reduce the likelihood of unnecessary contact or bumping. Coaches can have a predetermined safe or quiet space for individuals with SPD.

For visual stimulation, the coach may consider the clutter that appears in spaces surrounding the athletes. Understandably, reducing clutter and organizing in some places can be challenging. However, during team talks, chalk or white boards can be kept clean and free of unnecessary information, with simple messages. Outdoors, an available bin for quick storage of unused equipment may help keep the practice areas free of distracting materials from one phase of practice to the next.

© Rena Schild/Shutterstock.

With auditory stimulation, coaches may give athletes notice when loud noises (e.g., whistles, buzzers, etc.) may be used for any given day or drill, or consider if the use of excessive noise is crucial.

There are also considerations when managing the practice environments. An environment that is similar to "yesterday" is preferable for someone with SPD to one that is laden with changes and spontaneity. While there are certainly unavoidable or unanticipated changes in routine in sport, coaches may be careful to establish routines that can be relatively consistent and also be sure to give advance notice for broader changes in routine. For the underresponsive athlete who may be drawn to movement, consider having movement options. For instance, while talking to the team, perhaps stretching could occur simultaneously. In addition, coaches may consider how small group activities may be helpful as it may allow the coach to introduce incentives to strive for (which can be helpful) and an opportunity to pair the athlete with SPD with teammates who are also good role models.

Coaches may also help athletes with SPD become more organized. A coach may consider ways to simplify messages and material, including making eye contact when communicating, being concise and specific, and repeating information if necessary. Using a variety of ways to communicate messages may be helpful, including direct speaking, writing, drawing, and demonstrating. The athlete may also be asked to repeat instructions for understanding. Breaking down information and tasks into manageable units may be helpful. It can help the athlete "see the end" of a task and present more opportunities for success. Coaches may create and distribute basic weekly or monthly schedules with planned activities and expectations. These may include areas to "check off" what has been completed.

In terms of adapting one's own behavior, coaches may anticipate that an athlete with SPD may not follow the same trajectory with athletic development their peers do. Coaches may make a point to respect the athlete's sensory needs and offer alternatives and adjustments to allow them to feel safe. Coaches may emphasize the positive aspects of what the athlete has accomplished, helping assure them and support their sense of competence. If or when an athlete with SPD does not complete a task or develop a motor skill in the same way or speed peers may have, participation, effort, and process may still be emphasized and rewarded. Together, the sport environment can be a safe place in which the athlete develops a solid sense of competence and self-esteem.

VIGNETTE Part Two

Pat called Nika into the office for a chat. That no-slide had really bothered her, but there were other things that bothered her too. Nika walked up to the office and almost seemed to hesitate before knocking on the side of the door.

"Hi Nika, come on in."

"Hi Coach." Nika looked down. "You wanted to see me?"

"Yes, thanks for coming in. I was just curious why you didn't slide into second the other afternoon. I think most players would have, but you didn't."

"Well..." Pat waited for several seconds. "It's hard to explain but I just don't like sliding."

"Now that you mention it, and I know it's still early in the season, but I don't know that I've ever seen you slide. What is it about sliding that you don't like?"

"Well..."

"I promise I'm not upset. I just want to understand. Is it that you've never been taught how to slide?"

"Well, I don't like getting dirty and messy," Nika finally blurted out.

That was not what Pat was expecting but tried not to show surprise. There must be something more to this.

"I see. So, tell me, are there other things that bother you like getting dirty? Again, you're not in trouble. I'm just trying to figure out how I can help you be better."

"Well, I mean, it bothers me when things in the dugout are messy. I can't concentrate on the game. And then when everyone shouts and screams, it bothers me a lot too."

Pat began to see that this wasn't something as simple as technique. It was time to talk with the school counselor and Nika's teachers to find out if they were noticing anything similar.

Additional Resources

- Auer, C. R., & Auer, M. M. (2010). *Making sense of your senses: A workbook for children with sensory processing disorder*. New Harbinger Publications.
- Kranowitz, C. (2006). *The Out-of-Sync Child Has Fun, Revised Edition: Activities for Kids with Sensory Processing Disorder*. New York: Penguin.

- STAR Institute: https://www.spdstar.org/
- Understood: https://www.understood.org/en/learning-thinking-differences/child-learning-disabilities/sensory-processing-issues/understanding-sensory-processing-issues

Summary

- SPD, sometimes also referred to as sensory integration dysfunction, is the inability to process information received through one or more of the senses. The dysfunction occurs in the central nervous system, including the brain, which is unable to efficiently process, organize, and analyze (i.e., integrate) sensory messages.
- One in 20 individuals (5%) or more may be impacted by SPD.
- Individuals with SPD may be under- or over-responsive to environmental stimuli.
- The processing difficulties can learn to challenge in adaptive, academic, and motor learning areas, including athletics.
- Coaches may consider:
  - Reducing sensory overload (where applicable)
  - Managing practice environments
  - Helping the athletes become more organized
  - Adapting one's own behavior

Questions for Consideration

1. What are three examples of someone exhibiting signs of SPD?
2. What does interoception mean, and how does it apply to someone with SPD?
3. T/F: An athlete with SPD needs a more structured, disciplinarian approach.
4. Explain how you might reduce sensory overload for an athlete with SPD in your sport.
5. Give three examples of how you might adjust your own behavior when coaching an athlete with SPD.

References

Kranowitz, C. S., & Archer, E. (1998). *The out-of-sync child*. Berkley Publishing Group.

Miller, L. J., Fuller, D. A., & Roetenberg, J. (2014). *Sensational kids: Hope and help for children with sensory processing disorder (SPD)*. Penguin.

CHAPTER 7

Sensory Conditions—Visual

VIGNETTE Part One

"Green, sandwich, google, horse." Asher Boltan quietly spoke into his headset from a spotter's box high up in the stadium. It was a beautiful, sunny afternoon for football, and his team was in an intense back-and-forth battle midway through the second quarter. Down on the football field, the message was relayed and the boards for the next play were held high for his offense to see. The play called for play action pass, where the primary target was his tight end Henry Floki, who would initially block before slipping into the flat, and then turning back to the quarterback for the catch. The play worked beautifully, and Floki gained eight yards on the catch before dragging a couple of defenders for another three. Asher made a mental note to keep that one in reserve for later in the game. Floki had soft hands, knew how to sell a block, and was one of his most reliable third down go-to players.

The struggle for both teams continued as the day faded into night. Now deep into the fourth quarter, Asher's team was up by two, and he knew a strong drive now could seal the game. With a third down and six, Boltan called down for "green, sandwich, google, horse" again. The quarterback took the snap, faked to his tailback, and flicked the ball toward Floki. But Floki turned upfield, not back to the quarterback, and Asher watched in horror, then relief came, as a linebacker dropped what should have been an easy pick. Floki shook his head as he trotted off the field, making way for the punt team.

Forms, Definitions, and Prevalence

Visual conditions, including blindness, involves multiple definitions and describes a range of capabilities. For instance, the legal definition of blindness is based upon a clinical assessment of visual acuity. Part of the clinical assessment is the standard reading of letters on a chart (with lines and letters of varying sizes). Individuals are considered legally blind when they can only read the top line (size 200)—using both eyes *and* with corrective lenses on—from 20 feet. They may be diagnosed as legally blind with 20/200 acuity. As a point of reference, average visual acuity is 20/20, describing those who can see the size 20 line from 20 feet away.

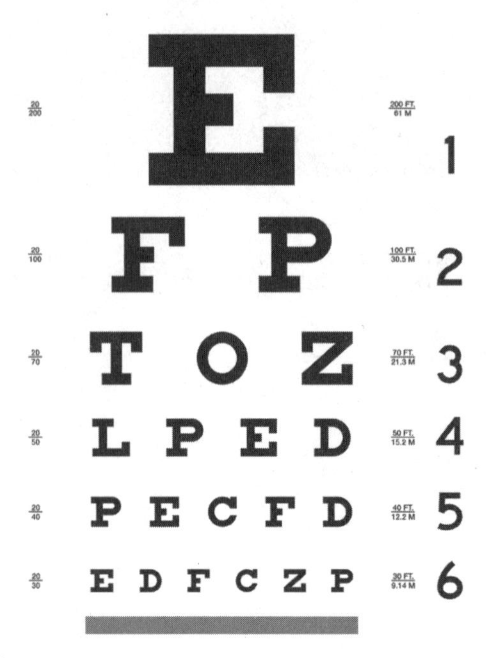

© Germán Ariel Berra/Shutterstock.

Individuals may also be legally blind with average acuity if their field of vision is impaired, which is referred to as *tunnel vision*. Thus, one can be legally blind but still have some degree of vision. The legal definition of blindness is used to determine eligibility for programs or services and does not categorically indicate that someone has total loss of vision (Turnbull et al, 2013).

The Individuals with Disabilities Education Act (IDEA) defines visual disability as "an impairment in vision that, even with correction, adversely affects a child's educational performance. The term includes both partial sight and blindness." (sec. 300.8). While visual impairments/conditions or disabilities interfere with vision, these individuals still may experience the world in visual ways. There are those with *low vision*, who can generally read printed material and see things in their field of vision but may need optical aids to do so optimally. These individuals still rely on vision for learning. Those with low vision are not necessarily legally blind. There are those who are *functionally blind* who primarily use braille for reading and writing. They may have some vision but may use it to supplement the tactile and auditory senses, which they primarily use for learning. There are also those who are *totally blind*, who do not receive meaningful visual information and use other senses to gather environmental information and learn. Atypical development of or damage to any part(s) or the visual system (see **Figure 7.1**) can impair how an individual is able to process visual stimuli.

In addition to visual acuity or field of vision, other conditions can impact visual capabilities, including *lack of binocular vision, amblyopia* (lazy eye), and *color blindness*. Descriptions of each are as follows:

- **Binocular vision** refers to the coordinated functioning of both eyes. Given that they are positioned inches apart, each eye has a slightly different view, but

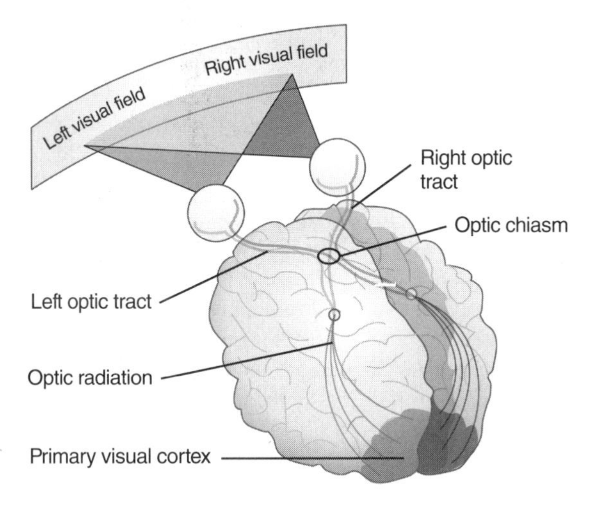

Figure 7.1 The visual system.

the brain combines these viewpoints into one image. This combined image also supports our ability to see things in three dimensions (3-D). A binocular vision condition is evident when the eyes are unable to coordinate in such a way, which negatively impacts depth perception. One such condition that can cause binocular vision impairment is strabismus, when one eye may wander or move in different directions than the other. However, binocular vision may be difficult to detect because the straying of one eye may not be consistent.

- **Amblyopia (lazy eye)** is a type of binocular condition. It is also called "lazy eye" referring one weaker eye and a stronger eye, which may function normally. As much as 3% of children may have amblyopia. With amblyopia, there is a neurological disconnect between the brain and one eye, causing difficulty in the brain receiving, processing, and recognizing information received from that eye. In short, one eye and the brain are not working together properly. Without treatment, the brain may begin to "work around" the weaker eye and turn off signals to rely more strongly on the other eye. The vision loss may cause children to squint, tilt their head, or shut one eye as they try to see something. It can also cause poor depth perception. Amblyopia can be caused by nearsightedness, farsightedness, or astigmatism in which the issue is worse in one eye than the other. It can also be caused by strabismus (when one eye may turn up, down, in, out, or wander) or droopy eyelids. These pre-existing conditions may cause amblyopia but are not telltale signs. For example, someone with amblyopia will not necessarily have eyes that do not move in synchrony in the same direction. Early identification is key (through screenings) and treatment can be effective long-term in retraining the eye(s) (Boyd, 2020).
- The American Academy of Ophthalmology (AAO) describes **color blindness** as an inability to see colors in a typical way, making it difficult to distinguish among colors. In the eye, cells that are sensitive to the colors of lights (called

cones) may be absent or not working properly in cases of color blindness. With mild color blindness, people can see color(s) accurately in bright light but have more difficulty in poor light. With moderate color blindness, certain color(s) are not seen in any light intensity. With mild and moderate color blindness, the sharpness (acuity) of vision is not typically impacted. With severe color blindness, all color cones are absent, and everything is seen in shades of grey. This severe form is uncommon, although color blindness tends to remain stable through life. The AAO notes that the term color blindness can be misleading in that most individuals (mild or moderate cases) see many colors clearly and do not live in a world of grey images. As such, it may impact day-to-day activities minimally. The AAO notes that the test for color blindness is rather simple; viewing a set of images is one of the most reliable tests. In **Figure 7.2**, there are numbers embedded in dots of color. The numbers are a different color than the rest of the dots and if someone cannot see those colors, they may be colorblind (Rauch, 2017; Turburt, 2021).

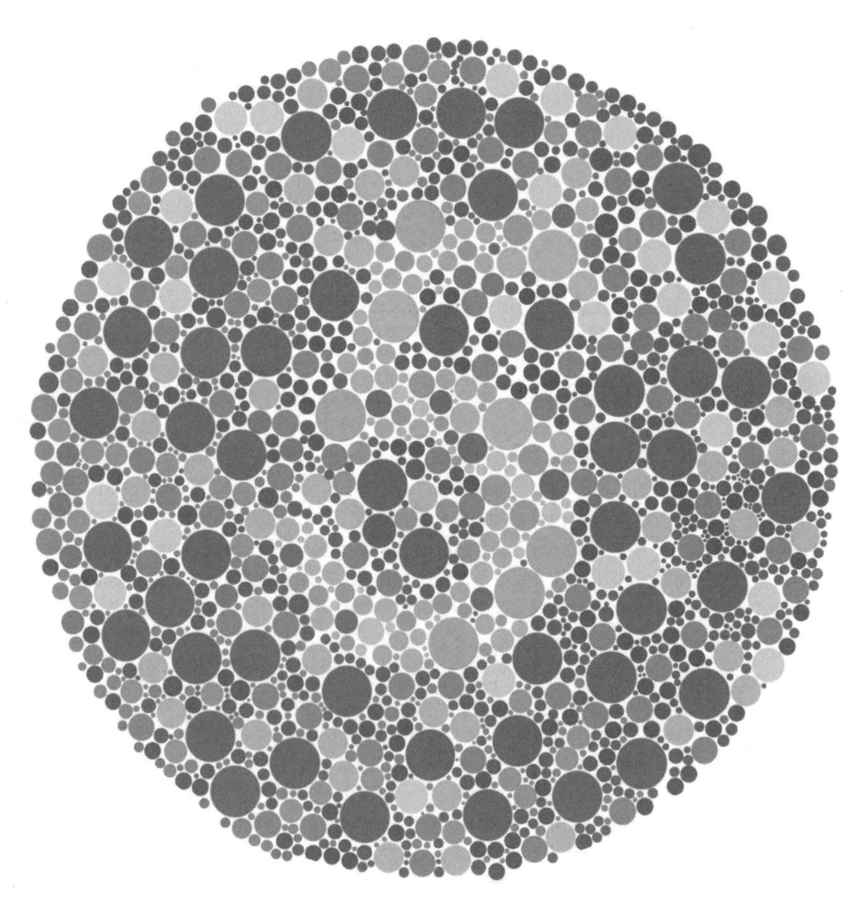

Figure 7.2 The multi-color dot/number test. The actual image is in color, with the number 5 in the center appearing green/blue, and the surrounding areas appearing red/orange/yellow.

How Visual Conditions Are Recognized

Some damage to visual systems can be *congenital*, or present from birth. For these individuals, low vision or lack of vision can impact their earliest experiences and access to environmental information. In other cases, individuals have *adventitious* visual conditions in which reduced vision occurs after birth. This may be due to an issue that presents itself later or some form of trauma. While even some time with vision and typical development can be extremely beneficial, all individuals with visual conditions have difficulties with *incidental learning*. This type of learning occurs without direct or explicit instruction—the individual "stumbles" into experiences with the environment and subsequently can embrace preexisting visual experiences and memory (e.g., in home, school, books, playgrounds) to help form ideas and understanding of things. So, for infants and young children with visual conditions, they may benefit from having extra time to interact with their environment, including from close distances to get better mental images or through feeling objects.

Low vision can limit the range of experiences an individual engages in, the ability to get around safely or spontaneously (perhaps particularly in new environments), and the frequency of social interactions. In turn, these limited experiences can impact academic learning, social skills, motivation, and motor skill development. In educational settings, there are many accommodations that may be made to support progress and inclusivity. Coaches may also make some basic considerations and accommodations.

Implications for Sport Participation and Performance

Children with visual conditions tend to experience less physical activity than their peers (Wrzesińska et al, 2018). Coaches can be important figures in making physical activity and sport friendly, enjoyable, and accessible for these athletes. Coaches can also help athletes overcome some of the barriers that they face when it comes to exploration and participation of sport.

Visual difficulties can impact motor development and learning. In addition, reduced or low vision is also clearly linked with sport play, including how athletes detect and process movement (i.e., themselves, teammates and opponents, and objects) or color, perceive depth, as well as communicate with others (i.e., coaches, teammates). For instance, traditional coach-athlete or athlete-athlete communication may rely on nonverbal gestures, body language, or cues and signals during play. These would become difficult or impossible with athletes with impaired vision.

Having reduced or no vision is one of the conditions recognized by the Paralympics for sport classification. For instance, goalball is a Paralympic sport reserved exclusively for athletes who are *only* visually impaired—those athletes having 10% or less of visual acuity, or whose visual field (tunnel vision) is a 40-degree diameter or less.

Several adaptations are made in goalball. All players wear eyeshades (and sometimes eye patches) to ensure no athletes can see during game play. Teams are composed of six players, three of whom play at one time. The object is to move a ball—which weighs 2.8 pounds and contains small bells that create sounds when in motion—along the ground and past opponents into a net to score, with opposing players using their entire bodies to defend their goal. All players are on their hands, knees, or feet during competition. String is attached to court markings to allow players to feel court lines and orient themselves on the court. Goalball made its Paralympic debut in 1976 in Toronto and has become extremely popular. The level of vision required for this game is akin to legal blindness. Game play is facilitated and guided by auditory sensations. Recent research has indicated that lack of vision may lead to enhanced audio-spatial capabilities (Battal et al., 2020).

Coaching Techniques and Strategies

Coaches may more commonly encounter athletes with low vision, or perhaps some cases of functional blindness. Modifications to the sport itself do not occur in these cases; however, coaches and athletes may benefit from making some adjustments to enhance communication and performance. Larsen (2014) demonstrated the use and effectiveness of a multistep mental skills training program designed specifically for athletes with visual difficulties, and to enhance communication in instances where nonverbal gestures and cues are difficult. Coaches may consider:

- How much they use nonverbal communication.
- How much visual information the athletes can process, and if alternatives are available.

- Adapting communication and instructional methods further by considering how to modify printed materials (if used).
- Augmenting instruction with other experiences.
- Opportunities for assisted technology.

Athletes with low vision may use or require optical devices such as glasses or magnifying glasses to read printed material (e.g., cue cards, playbooks, schedules, etc.). Coaches should plan to make sure athletes with low vision have the same opportunities to read printed material they may require of the athletes on the team, both within and outside of competition.

Coaches should also keep in mind that athletes with low vision may have difficulty understanding movement and sport skills and concepts given that they are not necessarily able to view images, diagrams, videos, or demonstrations in the same way their peers do. Such images offer important contextual cues and vicarious learning, and without them, coaches should be prepared to offer more experiential activities to support understanding and learning. Perhaps more so than academic settings and topics, coaches may be well-equipped in sport settings to integrate tactile and kinesthetic experiences into learning activities. To illustrate, a coach demonstrating a sport skill should follow up by having athletes walk through key stages of the skills, being particularly aware to have the athlete(s) with low vision participate in such incidental learning. While sense of touch is not a complete substitute for visual information, many sport-related objects can be understood better through tactile experience, giving the athlete time to experience them.

There are cases where some sport modifications will be necessary due to visual conditions. Lieberman and Childs (2020) made a "modifications checklist" for a variety of sport and events that coaches could consider. This list would be useful

for dialogue with an athlete, but also if a coach is advocating for the athlete with administrators.

Lieberman & Childs (2020) offered some useful guidelines for sport accommodation for individuals with visual conditions. For any sport, coaches may introduce spaces and equipment by permitting athletes to experience them in a tactile sense. Coaches may also use tactile modeling and physical guidance for skill introduction and development. They may also inquire with athletes about their preferences for equipment and accommodations. Some more sport-specific suggestions include:

- Baseball (beep)
  - Rubber tee
  - Batting gloves with Velcro
  - Consistent pitch technique (for live pitch hitting)
  - Carpet squares or poly spots (for hitting stance)
  - Guide runners for base running
  - Verbal cues for game and simulation
- Athletics/Track and Field
  - Running events
    - Guide runner
    - Guidewire or tether running
    - Talking pedometer or playlist to track time/distance
    - Clapping to signal pace (fast, slow)
    - Music to indicate direction
  - Jumps
    - Thick mats for landing
    - Guide wire through take off area
    - Clapping or beeper for direction or pace
    - Step counting to take off point
  - Throws
    - Hula hoop for throwing circle
    - Mats for stance
    - Auditory cues for direction
- Biking
  - Bright fluorescent lines
  - Lead biker with bright apparel
  - Spotters (on either side of biker)
  - Audible cues or music to indicate direction
  - Balance or tandem bike
- Swimming
  - Physioball or bench to teach technique on deck
  - Goggles
  - Different audible sounds at different ends of pool
  - Sprinkler to indicate end of lane
  - Lane lines
  - Tapper (stick with tennis ball or part of pool noodle on end)
- Gymnastics
  - Tactile modeling for technique
  - Spotters
  - Audible cues for take off areas (vault) and corners of floor mat
  - Carpet squares to indicate positioning

- Basketball
  - Use cane or stick to feel backboard and rim
  - Begin with two-handed dribbling technique
  - Begin with alternate point system (e.g., 1.0 = hitting net; 2.0 = hitting backboard; 3.0 = hitting rim; 4.0 = hitting square on backboard; 5.0 = making basket).
  - Human guide during game
  - Audible cues and midcourt and end lines (Lieberman & Childs, 2020).

The above list is not an exhaustive in terms of sport or modification ideas. There may be room for coaches and athletes to be creative in how to utilize equipment and adapt sport environments. As one of the "universal approaches" in the above list indicates, open dialogue with athletes about their preferences is important.

VIGNETTE Part Two

A punt and field goal later, Asher's team found themselves down by a point, a fourth and five on their 42-yard line, with only 54 seconds to go. They had to get a first down and the clock was ticking! "Green, google, sandwich, horse," Asher called down to the sideline, relying on his trusted tight end for a first down. He held his breath as the play unfolded. As expected, Floki held his block beautifully before slipping out, sprinting a few steps and making his cut... upfield! Asher couldn't believe it as once again, the ball went underneath his reliable tight end. His quarterback stood there, head in hands, knowing the game was over.

Asher, likewise, couldn't believe Floki would have made the wrong turn twice. It was so unlike him. He watched as players came up to Floki and voiced their encouragement to him but walked away obviously disappointed. Floki, meanwhile, appeared to be having an argument with the signal caller. What was going on? Why was Floki angrily pointing at the green board? He'd have to get to the bottom of this.

Additional Resources

- American Foundation for the Blind: https://www.afb.org/
- American Printing House for the Blind: https://www.aph.org/
- United States Association of Blind Athletes (USABA): https://www.usaba.org/

Summary

- The Individuals with Disabilities Education Act (IDEA) defines visual disability as "an impairment in vision that, even with correction, adversely affects a child's educational performance. The term includes both partial sight and blindness." (sec. 300.8)
- Visual capabilities range from average vision to low vision to blindness.
  - Low vision, functional blindness, total blindness

- Vision, including the legal definition of blindness, can relate to visual acuity or field of vision.
- Other conditions impacting vision include:
    - Amblyopia (lazy eye), color blindness, lack of binocular vision
- Reduced vision is clearly linked with sport play, including how athletes detect and process movement (i.e., themselves, teammates and opponents, and objects) as well as communication with others (i.e., coaches, teammates).
- Coaches may consider how much they employ nonverbal communication, how much the athletes are able to process, and if alternatives are available.
- Coaches may consider adapting communication and instructional methods further by considering how to adapt printed materials (if used), augmenting instruction with other experiences, and opportunities for assisted technology.
    - Athletes with low vision should have the same opportunities to read printed material that coaches may require of the athletes on the team.
    - Coaches should be prepared to offer more experiential activities to support understanding and learning.

Questions for Consideration

1. Explain in your own words what a visual sensory impairment/condition is. Give examples.
2. Research color blindness and explain some of the colors that are most commonly an issue.
3. How can you determine whether someone has a visual difficulty in your sport? What would you look for? Could you test it without actually "testing it?"
4. Which coaching technique and strategy do you think would be hardest to adapt within your own sport. Why?
5. Are there any rules within your sport that would make it challenging for an individual with a visual condition? What adaptations in your sport already exist?

References

Battal, C., Occelli, V., Bertonati, G., Falagiarda, F., & Collignon, O. (2020). General enhancement of spatial hearing in congenitally blind people. *Psychological Science, 31*(9), 1129–1139. https://doi.org/0956797620935584.

Boyd, K. (2020). *Amblyopia: What is lazy eye?* https://www.aao.org/eye-health/diseases/amblyopia-lazy-eye

Individuals with Disabilities Education Act (2007). https://sites.ed.gov/idea/regs /b/a/300.8/c/13

International Paralympic Committee. (2016). *International standards for eligible impairments.* https://www.paralympic.org/sites/default/files/document/61004145727129_2016_10_04_International_Standard_for_Eligible_Impairments_1.pdf

International Paralympic Committee. (n.d.). *Goalball.* https://www.paralympic.org/goalball

Lieberman, L. J., & Childs, R. (2020). Steps to success: A sport-focused self-advocacy program for children with visual impairments. *Journal of Visual Impairment & Blindness, 114*(6), 531–537. https://doi.org/10.1177/0145482X20971960

National Eye Institute (2019). *Amblyopia.* https://www.nei.nih.gov/learn-about-eye-health/eye-conditions-and-diseases/amblyopia-lazy-eye

Rauch, K., Edmond, J. C. (2017). *How color blindness is tested.* https://www.aao.org/eye-health/diseases/how-color-blindness-is-tested

Wrzesińska, M., Lipert, A., Urzędowicz, B., & Pawlicki, L. (2018). Self-reported physical activity using International Physical Activity Questionnaire in adolescents and young adults with visual impairment. *Disability and Health Journal, 11*(1), 20–30.

Additional Readings

Gür, K., Beyhan, A., Aktan, Ç., Akbulut, E., Sezer, M., Çelik, Ş., & Çakıcı, T. (2020). Physical activity levels, enjoyment, and perceptions of barriers to physical activity of adolescents with visual impairments in Turkey. *Journal of Visual Impairment & Blindness, 114*(6), 502–515.

Haegele, J. A., & Buckley, M. (2019). Physical education experiences of Alaskan youths with visual impairments: A qualitative inquiry. *Journal of Visual Impairment & Blindness, 113*(1), 57–67.

Larsen, C. H. (2014). Preparing for the European championships: A six-step mental skills training program in disability sports. *Journal of Sport Psychology in Action, 5*(3), 186–197. doi: 10.1080/21520704.2014.971989

McMahon, J., Emerson, R. S. W., Ponchillia, P., & Curtis, A. (2019). Measures of self-perception, level of physical activity, and body mass index of participants of sports education camps for youths with visual impairments. *Journal of Visual Impairment & Blindness, 113*(1), 43–56.

McMahon, J., Emerson, R. S. W., Ponchillia, P., & Curtis, A. (2019). Physical performance of participants of sports education camps for children with visual impairments. *Journal of Visual Impairment & Blindness, 113*(1), 32–42.

Turburt, D. (2021). What is color blindness? https://www.aao.org/eye-health/diseases/what-is-color-blindness

Turnbull, R., Turnbull, A., Wehmeyer, M. L., & Shogren, K. A. (2013). *Exceptional lives: Special education in today's schools* (7th ed.). Pearson.

CHAPTER 8

Sensory Conditions—Auditory

VIGNETTE Part One

The end of the third quarter had given coach Elisabeth Gronfeld the perfect opportunity to remind her team about a penalty corner play they have been practicing. The team has been awarded several PCs in the 3rd quarter, but they hadn't scored from any. Elisabeth Gronfeld called her 2-minute timeout at the perfect time. With a penalty corner coming, it gave her the opportunity to draw up a play she'd been thinking about for some time. Early in the collegiate season, she wanted to work out a few practice plays that would be useful later in the season. With a decent lead, now was the time to convert an idea on the pitch into reality on the scoreboard. As her players trotted over to her, she grabbed her small whiteboard and began to prepare. Her team gathered around her.

"Okay guys, we're doing great today, and I want to try something we've been putting in on the practice field but haven't tried yet in a game. On the next PC, I want to run Wide Right Fake. Let's run through it again really quickly."

Gronfeld looked down to draw out her plan as she spoke, but her marker wasn't in the mood. "Strike one for not being prepared," she chastised herself before putting down the whiteboard.

"Okay, forget the whiteboard. I'll just remind you all anyway. James, as the injector, I want you to push it out wide right to Zach, who is going to pass it straight back to you. From there, I want you to pass it back to Brent who'll come in and fake the shot, letting the ball go past to Jaime who'll take the shot. Got it everyone?"

Gronfeld looked up, made eye contact with the key players, but Jaime, her sweeper, didn't seem to be paying attention.

"Jaime," Gronfeld said sharply. Jaime was looking at something on the ground.

"Jaime!" Gronfeld said, much louder this time.

Jaime looked up startled.

"Yes, Coach?"

"You've got this?"

"Yes, Coach."

"Good. Okay everyone, let's give this a try."

With a last swig of their sports drinks, the players took to the field for their penalty corner. It worked beautifully at first. James to Zach to James to Brent to fake to... where was Jaime? Gronfeld put her hands to her head as Jaime stood immobile at the circle, and watched a defender break up the play. What had happened? Why hadn't Jaime played his part?

Forms, Definitions, and Prevalence

Hearing is assessed in terms of loudness and pitch. Loudness refers to the sound wave pressure detected by the ear (see **Figure 8.1**) while pitch is related to the frequency of sound vibrations. Increases in pressure and frequency would subsequently result in perceived loud noises and pitches of incoming sound. For individuals with hearing loss, ear function does not process and perceive sound in the same way. There are several identifiers for the degree of hearing loss, ranging from normal, to moderate, to profound, with additional identifiers in between.

Beyond normal hearing—when there is no recognizable impact on communication—a slight hearing loss would be evident when faint speech is difficult in noisy environments. Mild hearing loss is when faint speech is difficult even in quiet environments. When moderate hearing loss is present, conversational sounds are only detected at close distances. Group activities and discussions are challenging. In moderate-to-severe levels of hearing loss, only loud, clear speech can be detected. For these individuals, their speech is understandable, but impaired. When hearing loss reaches a severe level, speech cannot be heard unless it is very loud and even then, many words are not detected. Environmental sounds can sometimes be heard, although not necessarily quickly identified with regard to their source or location. Finally, when hearing loss is at a profound level, conversation cannot be heard. The individual's ability to speak is also impaired, typically difficult to understand, and may not be developed.

More than 20 million individuals (over 8%) in the United States have some form of hearing loss. In addition, approximately 20% of children who

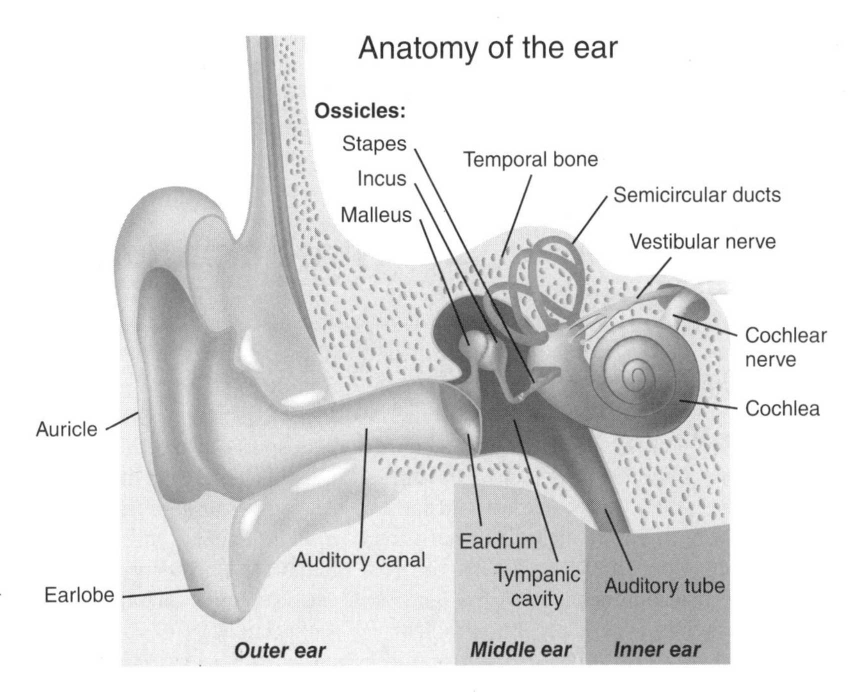

Figure 8.1 The ear.

are deaf or hard of hearing have another disability. Individuals who are hard of hearing or deaf typically communicate through oral speech (depending on level of hearing loss), American Sign Language and finger spelling, or simultaneous communication, which involves a combination of various forms of communication.

How Auditory Conditions Are Recognized

Hearing loss can be *prelingual* (i.e., before a child has learned language) or *postlingual* (i.e., after a child has begun to engage in spoken language). Most children (greater than 90%) who are deaf or hard of hearing have prelingual hearing loss, which may be attributed to premature birth or birth complications (which can impact the structural and/or functional aspects of the ear), heredity, or maternal rubella, which also impacts prenatal development. Prelingual hearing loss would typically be assessed by the early hearing screenings given shortly after birth and through infancy.

For people who are deaf or hard of hearing, learning language is perhaps the greatest challenge. This can impact the child socially and academically. It can be a challenge for hearing parents or guardians with a deaf child to learn new communication styles. Language and communication are the basis for many developmental activities, including storytelling, socializing, and nurturance. In school situations, it appears that inclusive environments in which the students can be in general education settings are best for academic achievement. However, if teachers are unable to communicate effectively with students who are deaf or hard of hearing, the ability to understand rules and concepts and engage in social activities can be difficult. While some challenges may be present, there are considerations and accommodations that can foster self-esteem and academic achievement. The same may be said for athletic participation and performance.

Implications for Sport Participation and Performance

Hearing conditions alone are not one of the eligible categories for Paralympic sport participation. However, the International Committee of Sports for the Deaf (ICSD) organizes the Deaflympics and other World Deaf Championships recognized by the International Olympic Committee. The sports in the Deaflympics mirror those in the Olympics and Paralympic Games. Beyond the elite level of competition, athletes who are deaf and hard of hearing are undoubtedly represented broadly in sport, including youth, recreational, amateur, and collegiate levels. To the latter, there are universities (e.g., Gallaudet University) designed specifically to accommodate deaf and hard of hearing students, including those who participate in athletic programs and compete collegiately.

While being deaf or hard of hearing does not impact athletic capabilities alone, there are ways in which audible processes are critical in play. For instance, coaches may frequently offer feedback verbally or give verbal instructions during competition. Also, during competition, teammates may communicate verbally, and officials may use their voices or audible devices (e.g., whistles, starting pistols, etc.) to direct athletes. Coaches may observe athletes who are hard of hearing not actively participating in collaborative activities, seeming to miss things people are saying and appearing to not understand some directions, or otherwise appear bored or inattentive at times because they are not hearing all that is said. Coaches should maintain the same level of performance expectations for athletes who are deaf or hard of hearing as they do for hearing athletes. However, there are considerations and techniques that may be undertaken by coaches to help facilitate learning, enjoyment, and achievement for these athletes.

Coaching Techniques and Strategies

In the 2020 Texas state high school football season, the Texas School for the Deaf Rangers (located in Austin) won their state championship. The coaches use a drum from the sidelines to call the plays and to count the cadence, so players know when to snap the ball and begin moving. Athletes can feel the vibrations of the noisy drumbeats across the field of play (TexasHSFootball.com, 2020). This example illustrates one way coaches considered athlete needs with specific sport demands and came up with a creative solution. There are numerous basic ways coaches can assist athletes who may have difficulty hearing.

One of the first things coaches can do is consider the extent of hearing loss in their respective athlete(s). Even if athletes wear devices such as hearing aids, they may not be able to wear them when they anticipate sweating, such as during practice and competitions. Another primary issue to consider is the degree to which the athlete and their family are open to accommodations. Deafness may be viewed as a linguistic and ethnic culture and coaches may benefit from taking time to learn the athlete's family and background as well as their preferences when it comes to accommodations. If applicable, the coach can also consider:

- The ways in which verbal and audible information is typically used in practice and competition.
- For some athletes who can still hear conversational speech, coaches may need to speak clearly, loudly, and distinctly.
- For athletes with more severe hearing loss, the coach may consider other communicative options and aids.
- Creating visual supports such as charts, signs, or images.
- Creating written versions or handouts of some material. For instance, early in a season, the team rules, expectations, and schedules may be written down and disseminated.
- Coaches may also create a list of technical terms or "jargon"—particularly new terms—which athletes can expect to hear introduced and used.
- Discuss with the athlete any situations they may not feel comfortable in, such as running along roadsides or trails should they not be able to hear approaching vehicles, bikes, or people.

Coaches may need to reinforce understanding of the information they are trying to communicate to the athlete and be open to finding individualistic ways in which communication will work best (e.g., being near the athlete when speaking,

amplifying voice, making eye contact, etc.). Coaches may also benefit from repeating and paraphrasing information. The coach could ask the athlete to sit near the front of the group when speaking and coaches may avoid speaking with their back to the athlete or team. Some individuals who are deaf or hard of hearing also lip read to support their understanding. Coaches may consider the lighting available to allow athletes to do so. Darkened meeting rooms may inhibit their ability to lip read. In addition, background noise could be minimized to the extent possible.

In some contexts, such as for coaches at schools and universities, they may reach out to see if interpreters are on campus and able to attend some practice times during the week to facilitate communication. This individual could also guide the coach and athlete(s) toward some basic communication patterns and help prepare the athlete(s) for upcoming events or changes to the routine.

VIGNETTE Part Two

Following the game, Elisabeth Gronfeld watched a video replay again on the long bus ride home. Most of the players had dozed off by now, but she had work to do. While there was a lot to cover, she wanted to go over Wide Right Fake. Again and again she watched, noting Jaime's failure to move. She hadn't said anything after the game, as she didn't want to criticize a player in front of other teammates, but it was clear Jaime hadn't been listening while she went over the play. But, to have not even moved means Jaime hadn't heard his name the first time she mentioned it, which was odd. She leaned across the aisle to her assistant coach, Jamil.

"Hey Jamil," she said quietly. "Did you notice how Jaime didn't even move to the ball on that PC?"

"Yeah," responded Jamil. "It was like he didn't hear any of the instructions."

"I know, right? I mean, he said he understood when I called him on it, but I really had to shout to get his attention. Have you noticed anything before?"

"Well, yeah. Now that you mention it, if I don't speak loudly during practice or I'm talking while looking at the screen during film time, I sometimes see him asking someone else what I said."

"Hmmm.... I wonder." Gronfeld paused for a moment. She had a feeling she knew what was wrong. Maybe that empty whiteboard marker had solved a puzzle.

Additional Resources

- Deaflympics: https://www.deaflympics.com/
- Hearing Loss Association of America (HLAA): https://www.hearingloss.org/
- International Committee of Sports for the Deaf (ICSD): https://www.deaflympics.com/icsd
- Lauren Clerc National Deaf Education Center: https://www3.gallaudet.edu/clerc-center/tips-to-go/tips-to-go-bookmarks—supporting-educational-success/accommodating-deaf-and-hard-of-hearing-students-in-schools.html
- National Association of the Deaf: https://www.nad.org/about-us/

Summary

- Hearing is assessed in terms of loudness and pitch. Briefly, loudness refers to the sound wave pressure detected by the ear, while pitch is related to the frequency of sound vibrations.
- More than 20 million individuals (over 8%) in the United States have some form of hearing loss.
- Hearing loss can be prelingual or postlingual.
- Hearing loss ranges:
    - Normal hearing—when there is no recognizable impact on communication.
    - Slight hearing loss—faint speech is difficult in noisy environments.
    - Mild hearing loss—faint speech is difficult even in quiet environments. Group activities and discussions are challenging.
    - Moderate-to-severe hearing loss—only loud, clear speech can be detected. Speech is understandable, but impaired.
    - Severe hearing loss—speech cannot be heard unless it is very loud; many words are not detected. Environmental sounds can sometimes be heard.
    - Profound hearing loss—conversation cannot be heard. The individual's ability to speak is also impaired.
- While being deaf or hard of hearing does not impact athletic capabilities alone, there are ways in which audible processes are critical in the course of play.
- Coaches may:
    - Consider the ways in which they typically rely on vocal and audible information to communicate with athletes.

- Consider the extent of hearing loss in their athletes.
- Consider the use of other communication tools and options.
- Write down some materials (e.g., team rules, technical terms)
- Enlist the support of interpreters to help guide communication and offer suggestions.
- Take precautions so that athletes are safe in all environments when hearing is impaired.

Questions for Consideration

1. What percentage of individuals in the United States have some form of hearing loss? Does this surprise you? Why/why not?
2. Most athletes will know if they are hard of hearing. What reasons might they disguise or hide it from you as coach?
3. Provide three strategies for helping an athlete who is deaf or hard of hearing.
4. Why might jargon be a problem and how can it be addressed?
5. What steps could you take in your own situation to help identify and/or work with an athlete who is deaf or hard of hearing?

References

International Paralympic Committee. (2016). International standard for eligible impairments. https://www.paralympic.org/sites/default/files/document/61004145727129_2016_10_04_International_Standard_for_Eligible_Impairments_1.pdf

Mowinski, A. H. (2021). #MyTri: Adjusting to hearing loss as a triathlete. *Triathlete.* https://www.triathlete.com/culture/people/mytri-adjusting-to-hearing-loss-as-a-triathlete

TexasHSFootball.com. (2020, December 12). Deaf football team wins first-ever Texas state football championship. https://texashsfootball.com/deaf-footballteam-wins-first-ever-texas-state-football-championship

© miodrag ignjatovic/Getty Images.

CHAPTER 9

Communication and Language Disorders

VIGNETTE Part One

Pamela Porter sat down at her desk and opened her laptop. Coaching virtually had its challenges, but she loved the opportunity to work with athletes from around the globe who otherwise wouldn't have an opportunity to work with someone as qualified and experienced as her. "Technology is amazing," she thought to herself as she began the connection.

Naomi Enriquez was a talented racquetball prodigy from Paraguay who was looking to break into the professional scene, and a coach in Paraguay had recommended Pamela as the person to help her professionalize her game. This didn't just include technique and strategy but also building a personal brand that would attract sponsors. Racquetball wasn't a big sport, and sometimes coaches had to do more than just coach. She clicked the connect icon and waited until Naomi appeared on the screen.

"Hola, Naomi. ¿Como estas?" said Porter, trying to make Naomi feel comfortable. The first few sessions were always hard to establish a connection, so Porter did all she could to make it relaxed, even if it meant speaking in broken Spanish.

"Bien, gracias. ¿Y usted?"

"Bien. Your national coach Pedro told me that you spoke good English. My Spanish is not very good so is it okay if I speak in English?"

"Yes."

"Okay, that's great." Porter started by covering some basic ground rules about the session and how she worked. After the paperwork was complete, she asked Naomi to talk a little bit about herself. But Naomi was reticent to talk and used only a few sentences. Sensing this could be a language barrier, Porter didn't think too much of it and closed out the first session, scheduling Naomi for a week later.

Forms, Definitions, and Prevalence

Communication disorders include difficulties in language, speech, and communication. Broadly, language includes the use of conventional system of symbols, including spoken words, sign language, writing, or pictures. Speech is the production of sounds (as in spoken language) and includes aspects of articulation, fluency, and voice. Communication includes verbal and non-verbal behaviors that are shared with another person. Difficulties in these areas negatively impact the ability to receive and understand information, as well as express information, feelings, and thoughts (American Psychiatric Association, 2013).

In the current edition of the Diagnostic and Statistical Manual of Mental Disorders (DSM-5), there are several specific communication disorders, including language disorder, speech sound disorder, childhood-onset fluency disorder (or stuttering), and social communication disorder. While some of the signs and symptoms of communication disorders may overlap with symptoms of other hidden disabilities and conditions, they are not otherwise attributed to those conditions. For instance, individuals with hearing loss may demonstrate reduced vocabulary and ability to put words together in sentences, but language disorder is not accounted for by a sensory conditions. Communication disorders may be comorbid (or co-existing) with other issues such as autism spectrum disorder or hearing loss, but not necessarily. These communication disorders can fit into their own set of criteria, primarily impacting language, speech, and communication (American Psychiatric Association, 2013). Below are brief summaries of their unique features.

- **Language disorder** is evident with persistent problems with acquiring and using language in a variety of ways, including spoken, written, and sign language. This typically results in reduced vocabulary, limited sentence usage, and difficulties connecting sentences to explain ideas and topics. Overall, the language and communication capabilities are significantly lower than what is expected for the individual's age. The language problems cannot be explained by hearing loss or other conditions or delays.
- **Speech sound disorder** is shown through difficulty with producing sounds. It can severely inhibit verbal communication. These difficulties can interfere with development in a variety of areas, including academically, socially, and occupationally.
- **Childhood onset fluency disorder** is also known as stuttering. There are disruptions in the typical fluency and timing of speech production. The problems typically are shown through frequent syllable and sound repetition (difficulty in producing singular words) as well as prolongation of sounds. Words are often broken apart and may be filled with silence or other audible sounds in between. Those with childhood onset fluency disorder may use simpler words to avoid difficult ones and demonstrate physical tension and frustration when expressing themselves.
- **Social communication disorder** is marked by difficulties communicating in social situations. Individuals may have difficulty in typical social situations, including greetings. Sometimes, communication may not "match" the situation, such as adjusting speech in inside versus outside settings, or with a peer versus an adult. Common social communications, like conversation and storytelling, may be challening (American Psychiatric Association, 2013).

One commonality among these is that the onset of symptoms tends to be in early developmental periods. Another common feature of the language disorders is a persistent difficulty in producing words and sentences to engage in the typical course of communication and dialogue. It is not necessarily a coach's role to know specifically the presence or severity of the disorder, but to know they exist and can impact the ways athletes are able to send or receive communication.

How Communication and Language Difficulties Are Recognized

Communication disorders can occur in the presence of other disorders, or also be explained by neurological problems, brain or vocal cord injury, substance or medication side effects, or other physical conditions (e.g., cleft lip or palate). The cause of communication disorders is often unknown. Children develop and master many aspects of speech and sound early on. By the age of 8, children can typically produce most sounds and syllables that make up the words of their native language. Up to that age, as seen in the CDC Developmental Milestones (please see Additional Resources at the end of this chapter), there are numerous developmental milestones involving language and communication that are evident to family members.

The communication difficulties can negatively impact academic performance. Approximately 5% of children and adolescents have a speech or language difficulty that requires academic accommodations, and about half of those students may have a specific learning disability, such as dyslexia.

Implications for Sport Participation and Performance

In some of the ways in which communication challenges have implications for sport participation and performance in the context of other hidden disabilities (e.g., autism spectrum disorder) and conditions (e.g., hearing loss), the same may be said for communication disorders. These athletes may become frustrated in instances where they need receptive (e.g., hearing directions or receiving feedback from coaches, understanding on-the-field communication between teammates) or expressive (e.g., directing teammates, calling plays) language. With some basic considerations and accommodations, sport can become a place for these athletes to practice valuable communication skills.

Coaching Techniques and Strategies

Athletes with language disorders may not express their thoughts, feelings, or needs explicitly. Beyond being aware that the communication or language difficulties exist, coaches can help athletes by:

- Being patient with the athlete and avoiding correcting speech difficulties.
- Modeling acceptance in team environments.
- Speaking directly and deliberately to the athlete.
- Using active listening skills by allowing time for responses and paraphrasing what was heard.
- Reducing unnecessary external noise when speaking with the athlete.
- Developing a signal that the athlete can use when they are not understanding or needing more time or clarity.
- Anticipating when new or more complex ideas or tasks may be presented and allocate time to communicate this to the athlete in creative ways.
- Using tactile cues or visual aids where appropriate.
- Expanding their utterances by taking what they did say and making a complete sentence. This provides the athlete with a more complex model of language to use.
    - For example, if an athlete says "over there" when asked where the best pass option was, the coach can elaborate by saying "The best pass option

was there. That is correct. That is exactly where you should have passed in that situation."

- Offering statements that seem to correspond with an athlete's nonverbal behavior.
  - For instance, if an athlete points to a certain teammate in response to a coach's question about a play option, the coach could respond with "Correct—the best option is to that receiver 10 yards downfield," Again, the coach is giving the athlete a model of words to use in the future.
- Offering athletes with language disorders opportunities to practice speaking in public situations.
  - Coaches could provide questions in advance so the athlete has time to practice and rehearse. In all cases of communication, athletes should feel that their communication and input is valued.

VIGNETTE Part Two

After several sessions, Coach Porter was impressed with Naomi's progress on the court but was concerned that Naomi was neither talking much nor giving her much information. Porter had been tasked with improving Naomi on and off the court, but it was the off-the-court improvements, or lack thereof, that concerned her. Coaching virtually was so much harder than in person, and adding a foreign language to that made it even harder.

But something else didn't seem right. Naomi was clearly intelligent, and when she spoke in English, she used correct grammar. But some of the words didn't sound right. They were right grammatically, but Naomi seemed to miss a letter or something. "Racquetball" sounded like "wacquetball" and "down the line," a racquetball term, sounded like "down the wine." Normally, this wouldn't be an issue for Porter. She understood Naomi pretty well, but with her potential for stardom, both in Paraguay and on the Ladies Professional Racquetball Tour, Naomi would need to speak in public, giving speeches, interviews, and the like. Porter wasn't sure what the problem was, but she knew she wasn't qualified to help. It was time to do some research.

Additional Resources

- American Speech-Language-Hearing Association: https://www.asha.org/
- CDC Developmental Milestones: https://www.cdc.gov/ncbddd/actearly/milestones/index.html
- Understood: https://www.understood.org/en/learning-thinking-differences/child-learning-disabilities/communication-disorders/what-are-language-disorders

Summary

- Communication disorders include difficulties in language, speech, and communication.
- In the DSM-5, there are a few specific communication disorders, including:
  - Language disorder
  - Speech sound disorder
  - Childhood-onset fluency disorder (or stuttering)
  - Social communication disorder
- Approximately 5% of children and adolescents have a speech or language condition that requires academic accommodation.
- Athletes with language disorders may not express their thoughts, feelings, or needs explicitly.
- To enhance communication and understanding, coaches may consider techniques covered in other units where language or communication was also impaired, such as ASD or hearing loss.
- In addition, coaches may model and facilitate language skills by:
  - Helping expand utterance and complete sentences
  - Supplementing their nonverbal language and gestures with statements
  - Giving preplanned opportunities for public speaking

Questions for Consideration

1. What are some examples of communication disorders you might see in your athletic population?
2. It is not necessarily a coach's role to know specifically the presence or severity of the disorder, but to know they _______ and can _______ the ways athletes are able to _______ or _______ communication.
3. T/F: Most communication disorders are diagnosed before the age of 12.
4. List five ways in which you can help an athlete with a communication disorder.
5. Giving athletes an opportunity to speak in public can create anxiety. How could you help ease this situation?

Reference

American Psychiatric Association. (2013). Communication Disorders. In *Diagnostic and statistical manual of mental disorders* (5th ed.).

PART 4

Muscular and Bone Issues

CHAPTER 10

Fibromyalgia

VIGNETTE Part One

Coach Peter Grouch walked into the coach's meeting fully prepared. It is how any international head coach, or any coach for that matter, should be, after all. He said a few greetings to his diverse group of coaches and staff and seated himself at the head of the table.

"Okay, everyone. Let's have a status update," he said quickly. He didn't like long meetings if he could help it. "Injuries, what have we got? He looked up from his agenda to his head athletic trainer, Brenda Stillwell, who looked down at her report.

"Well, we've still got Heather out in rehab for at least a couple of weeks with her strained MCL. Jen had tweaked a hamstring before she got here for training, but it looks like she'll be good to go for next weekend's match." Brenda paused, knowing the next statement was not going to be received well. She took a breath and looked down.

"So... Abby has been in for treatment again, complaining of a sore right leg and feeling tired." There were groans around the room. Coach Grouch put his hand to his face and slowly rubbed his temple. Heather had seen this expression before, and it wasn't a good sign. She continued.

"Apparently, Abby got tackled hard during practice and said that she's experiencing aching and feels tired all of the time. From our initial assessment, there doesn't appear to be anything seriously wrong, but we want to sit her out for at least a practice to see if there are further issues."

"I don't get it," said fitness coach Danielle Forside. "One day she's fit and the next she isn't. I promise you we're not overtraining them. She's doing the same workouts as everyone else."

"I know, I know," said Coach Grouch slowly. "Look, it's obvious to all of us at the table here that there are issues going on. We can't have one of the best players in the world spending most of her time in the training room when we need her on the pitch. What's going on, Brenda?"

Brenda shrugged. "I'm not sure, but something's up. Too many reoccurring injuries to be nothing. She's not someone who doesn't want to be out there or doesn't want to train. I think we all know that." There were some nods around the room before Brenda continued. "I went back through her health history, and I've even spoken to her college coach in general terms. Honestly, Abby didn't seem to be having these injury issues in college, so it's either overtraining or something else."

"Well, it's something else," Danielle said rather quickly, no doubt wanting to make sure her program wasn't questioned.

"Yes, I know. I know." Brenda responded. "But I think something's going on beyond just Abby faking injuries or not being tough. Coach, with your permission, I'd like to pull Abby out for a while and try to figure out what's going on."

Grouch paused, before nodding. "Okay, everyone. Let's assume Abby's out for the next match and plan accordingly. Okay what's next?"

Brenda sat back as the coaches began discussing other topics. Abby was a conundrum, and she had work to do.

Forms, Definitions, and Prevalence

Fibromyalgia is a common pain disorder that involves pain and tenderness in the body, including muscles, ligaments, and tendons. The pain is often described as a "dull ache." The pain can be throughout the body or seem to migrate from place to place. The intensity of the painful sensation can fluctuate over time. The pain is widespread in that it can exist in upper and lower regions of the body, as well as on both sides. It is possible that fibromyalgia is caused by neurological conditions in which the brain and nervous systems (see **Figure 10.1**) amplify pain, making the individual experience pain in heightened and lasting ways.

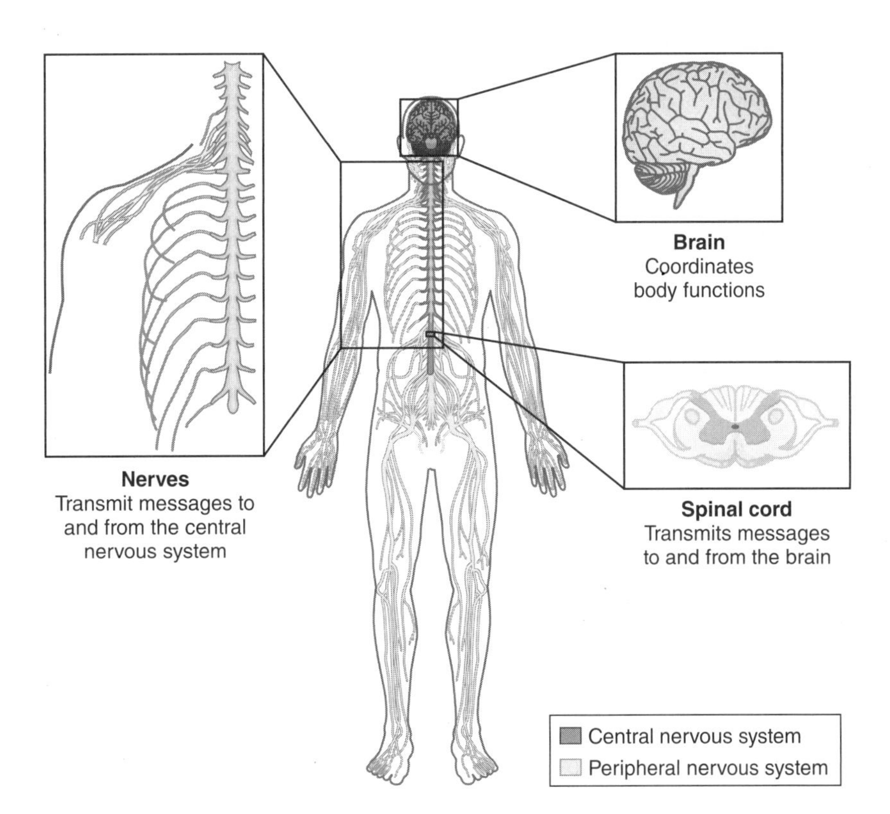

Figure 10.1 The central and peripheral nervous systems.

In the United States, as many as 10 million individuals may have fibromyalgia, making it one of the more common chronic pain conditions. The disorder can impact men, women, and children. However, most cases (75–90%) are female. There is no cure for fibromyalgia, although a combination of interventions and therapies can improve quality of life. Not only are there pharmacologic pain reducers but also a variety of psychological and behavioral therapies. Some of these therapies involve physical activity, including some aerobic exercise and yoga.

How Fibromyalgia Is Recognized

Fibromyalgia is most often diagnosed between the ages of 20 and 50, although the symptoms can emerge in childhood and adolescence. The painful symptoms of fibromyalgia may begin after triggering event(s), such as physical trauma and injury, surgery, infection, or extreme psychological stress. However, in other cases, the pain gradually builds up over time and cannot be traced to any event(s).

For some time, diagnosis of fibromyalgia has included a "tender point" exam, which assessed pain in a variety of areas on core quadrants of the body. Newer guidelines from the American College of Rheumatology do not require the tender point part of an exam, but there must be chronic (at least for 3 months) pain in at least four of five bodily areas:

- Left upper (shoulder, arm, jaw)
- Right upper (shoulder, arm, jaw)
- Left lower (hip, buttock, leg)
- Right lower (hip, buttock, leg)
- Axial (neck, back, chest, abdomen)

Beyond physical pain, there are other symptoms often associated with this chronic pain condition. Individuals with fibromyalgia may also report excessive fatigue, which may be partly due to painful aches disrupting prolonged bouts of sleep. Fibromyalgia often also has cognitive and psychological effects. For instance, the term "fibro fog" has been used to describe difficulty concentrating, keeping focus, and completing tasks. Those with fibromyalgia may also experience depressive symptoms and anxiety.

Implications for Sport Participation and Performance

The pain and potential lack of rest can negatively impact functioning in a variety of contexts, including home, school, work, and sport. The painful symptoms associated with fibromyalgia may make certain sport tasks particularly daunting or challenging. The pains that are typically associated with sport participation, including that which comes from physical exertion, soreness from physical training, or physical contact (e.g., bumping, tackling, etc.) may be amplified for individuals with fibromyalgia. Given the widespread nature of pain, even simpler movements (e.g., running, lunging, swinging, rotating, jumping) may be particularly painful (Inanıcı et al., 2010).

Cognitively, reduced ability to concentrate and complete tasks can negatively impact practice and communication. Moreover, some report problems with coordination, dizziness, and vision. Taken together, there are a variety of ways in which the symptoms of fibromyalgia (i.e., physical, cognitive, psychological) could impact sport participation and performance.

Coaching Techniques and Strategies

Some of the physical activity and supplemental activities involved in sport *can* have benefits for athletes with chronic pain conditions such as fibromyalgia. In addition, physical activity as part of a daily routine can help with sleep. However, each athlete will be unique in their experience and needs. So, coaches can enhance their understanding of the levels of pain that athletes with fibromyalgia symptoms may be experiencing, and maintain open dialogue regarding the tasks, activities, and position(s) the athlete feels they can perform on any given day.

Coaches and athletes should also have open dialogue with medical professionals close to the program, such as a team doctor or athletic trainer. These medical professionals are trained to help treat and prevent pain, including through physical or massage therapy.

Coaches can help make athletes aware of behavioral pain management techniques, as well as make them available. Through dialogue with athletes experiencing widespread, chronic pain and associated symptoms, coaches can be agents in pain management. Coaches may ask athletes what techniques—the ones with their doctor's approval—seem to help them reduce pain. The coach can consider ways in which these could be integrated on a daily or weekly basis. Coaches may also help athletes explore new ways to manage pain, although it should still fall within the scope of techniques approved by medical professionals.

Coaches can investigate which issues or experiences may enhance pain. For example, the time of day may impact pain. Individuals with fibromyalgia and chronic pain may report pain to be more intense in the morning. This is helpful information if coaches schedule morning workouts. According to the National Fibromyalgia Association (NFA), other factors that may make the pain worse include:

- Cold or humid weather
- Nonrestorative sleep

- Physical and mental fatigue
- Anxiety and stress
- Excessive physical activity or physical inactivity

As the last bullet point above suggests, individuals may have a "sweet spot" in terms of the amount and type of physical activity that they can handle or that is helpful for them in managing pain on a day-to-day basis. Coaches may be mindful of (and inquire about) which activities (e.g., weight training, strength work, drills) seem like "too much" for an athlete with fibromyalgia. The schedule for this athlete could be modified. The coach and athlete may have an agreed-upon signal indicating that something is too painful, and a break or assistance is needed. Other behavioral treatments that may be practical in sport settings include:

- Stretching
- Yoga
- Relaxation and breathing
- Aquatic workouts
- Massage

Some coaches may be well-versed in some of what appears in the list above. However, other professionals—in addition to the athlete's personal doctor—may help. Athletic departments may have athletic trainers and physical therapists to guide and assist with stretching or massage therapy before or after practice. Coaches may have access to swim instructors or pool facilities for guidance and supervision with water-based workouts.

Coaches may have access to wellness coordinators or sport psychologists to help with relaxation and breathing techniques. One particularly useful technique may be progressive muscle relaxation, which involves sequentially moving throughout the body and alternating between tensed and relaxed states in muscle groups. Coupled with controlled breathing, this can help reduce stress and pain. There are a variety of apps (e.g., *Calm, MyLife, Headspace*) that have breathing and relaxation scripts. A search engine (like Google) will also yield a variety of text- or video-based scripts that may be used. In addition, yoga may be a helpful supplemental activity (which can combine light physical activity, stretching, and breathing). Yoga can be adapted in a variety of ways to match the athletic and developmental capabilities of the athlete. Yoga instructors in the community may be willing to offer introductory sessions.

VIGNETTE Part Two

Later that day, Brenda was working on another athlete when Abby walked into the training room and flopped onto a training table. She let out an audible sigh. Brenda finished up with her athlete and walked over to Abby.

"How are things Abby?" Brenda asked.

"I'm so sick of hurting," Abby replied.

"Hurting from the tackle this morning?"

"Yes, but no. I mean, it feels like each day I'm sore somewhere new. It's so frustrating. I hate not being able to train. I'm letting down my team, my coaches, my country, everyone! I'm not fit. I'm not healthy. And I don't know why!" Abby was on the verge of tears.

"I hear you. I've done my own research based on what you've been telling me, and to be honest, I'm not sure what the problem is. I don't think it has anything to do with training though, so it's important to get help from an expert. I've talked with Coach Grouch and we'd like to have you do some tests and see a specialist. Is this something you'd be willing to do?

Abby looked to the floor and nodded quietly.

"Okay. Let's do that, find out what the problem is, and how we can tackle it together." Brenda put her arm around Abby and the sobbing started. Although Brenda's primary job was to keep players healthy for the national team, the care and well-being of the athlete was more important than anything else. She hated not being able to help an athlete, but sometimes you have to admit what you don't know and ask for help.

Additional Resources

- American College of Rheumatology (ACR): https://www.rheumatology.org/
- Fibromyalgia support community: https://www.inspire.com/groups/fibromyalgia/
- Mayo Clinic: https://www.mayoclinic.org/diseases-conditions/fibromyalgia /symptoms-causes/syc-20354780 National Fibromyalgia & Chronic Pain Association: https://fibroandpain.org/

Summary

- Fibromyalgia is a common pain disorder that involves pain and tenderness in the body, including muscles, ligaments, and tendons. The pain is often described as a "dull ache."
- In the United States, as many as 10 million individuals may have fibromyalgia, making it one of the more common chronic pain conditions. The disorder can impact men, women, and children. Most cases (75–90%) are female.
- Beyond physical pain, there are other symptoms often associated with this chronic pain condition. Individuals with fibromyalgia may also report:
  - Excessive fatigue, which may be partly due to painful aches disrupting prolonged bouts of sleep.
  - Cognitive and psychological effects, including "fibro fog" has been used to describe difficulty concentrating, keeping focus, and completing tasks.
  - Depressive symptoms and anxiety.
- The painful symptoms associated with fibromyalgia may make certain sport tasks particularly daunting or challenging.
- The pains that are typically associated with sport participation, including that which comes from physical exertion, soreness from physical training, or physical contact (e.g., bumping, tackling, etc.) may be amplified for individuals with fibromyalgia.

- Coaches and athletes should also have open dialogue with medical professionals close to the program, such as a team doctor or athletic trainer.
- Coaches can encourage, support, and make time for a variety of behavioral techniques to help prevent, reduce, and manage pain in athletes.

Questions for Consideration

1. What are some of the reasons fibromyalgia is hard to identify?
2. T/F: Fibromyalgia is most often found in males.
3. What is fibro fog?
4. List two physical and two other effects of the condition.
5. What are behavioral management techniques and how can they help?

Reference

Inanıcı, F., Özdemir, O., Aydoğ, T., Şendil, A., Kutsal, Y. G., & Hasçelik, Z. (2010). The frequency of fibromyalgia in sport professionals. *Rheumatology International*, *31*(8), 1121.

CHAPTER 11

Bone and Joint Diseases

VIGNETTE Part One

Coach Rueben Gonzalez watched as their opponent's third baseman blasted a pitch out to left field. "Easy catch," Gonzalez thought to himself, as the ball floated in the air toward Jensen Yonder. Thirteen-year-old Jensen Yonder made the catch, but his approach looked awkward, almost as if he was limping. Third out, next inning, and the outfielders made their way to the dugout.

Gonzalez watched Jensen walk in, and while Jensen didn't appear to be limping, something didn't seem right to him.

"Hey Jensen, nice catch. Way to move into position quickly and get that glove prepped."

"Thanks Coach."

"You okay out there? Seemed to be limping a little."

"I'm fine, Coach," Jensen said a little too quickly.

"You sure? Nothing hurting?"

"No Coach. I'm good."

"Okay. Well, let me know if anything's bothering you okay?"

"Yes Coach."

Gonzalez let it go but kept an eye on Jensen throughout the game. While Jensen was clearly trying to hide it, he was intuitively rubbing his right knee. He made a mental note to have a quick word with his dad after the game. As a club team, he did see Jensen often, but without an athletic trainer on staff or easily accessible, often, injuries and such were his responsibility. Because of this, he was hypervigilant about ensuring that his athletes were healthy.

Following the game, Gonzalez consoled his players on a tough loss, but reminded them of the good things they had done and the work they had put in. Baseball was a process, and it took time to develop as a player. As the team separated to their respective families, Gonzalez went looking for Jensen's dad.

"Hi Robert," Gonzalez said when he had located him among the many trying to leave. "May I have a quick word with you?"

"Sure, Coach. What's up?"

Gonzalez guided Robert over to the side for some privacy.

"Nothing serious. I just noticed Jensen limping a little and rubbing his right knee. I just wondered if you knew if he had an injury or something? I know he might not tell me because he could be worried that he might lose his spot on the team. That's the last thing on my mind. I just want to make sure he's healthy."

Robert shook his head. "No, I haven't noticed anything."

"Hmmmm... Okay. Well, would you let me know if you do notice anything. I'd rather you not share with Jensen that we talked, as I don't want him worrying about it, but if you do see something, let me know please?"

"Sure thing, Coach. Thanks for noticing."

With that, the conversation ended and Robert went to find Jensen.

Forms, Definitions, and Prevalence

There are some conditions that cause pain and swelling in joints and bones, which can cause subsequent discomfort and reduction of movement for athletes. Three of these are *arthritis, Osgood-Schlatter,* and *Sever's disease.*

Arthritis is related to swelling, tenderness, or pain in one or more joints. There are numerous types of arthritis. Together, arthritis is the leading cause of disability in the United States in cases in which it becomes intense enough to limit capacities and daily activities. It is estimated that over 50 million adults and 300,000 children and adolescents have some form of arthritis. The most common forms of arthritis are *osteoarthritis* and *rheumatoid arthritis. Osteoarthritis* occurs when cartilage (rubbery, connective tissue between joints) breaks down over time. *Rheumatoid arthritis* is when the immune system attacks the body's own tissue, including joints (see **Figure 11.1**). Both forms can have some of the same symptoms. Four of the core symptoms associated with arthritis are:

- Pain: Can be at rest or while moving, in one or more body parts.
- Stiffness: Which may be particularly bad in the morning or after long periods of being still (like sitting).
- Swelling: Skin around joint(s) can be swollen, red, or warm to the touch.
- Difficulty moving joint(s)

Another condition is Osgood-Schlatter disease, which involves pain and swelling below the kneecap. Internally, the growth plate above the shin is pulled on

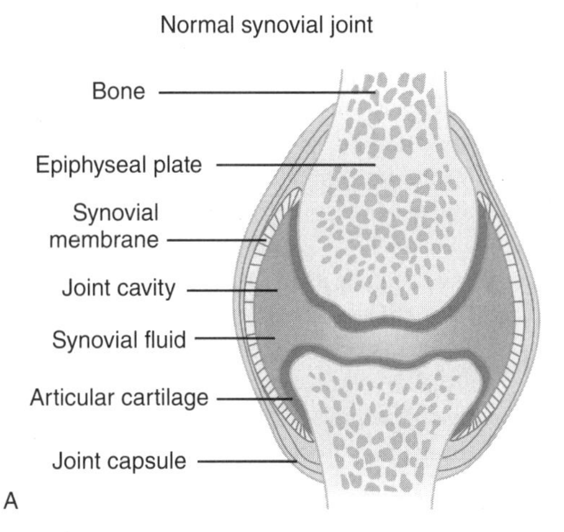

Figure 11.1 (Continued)

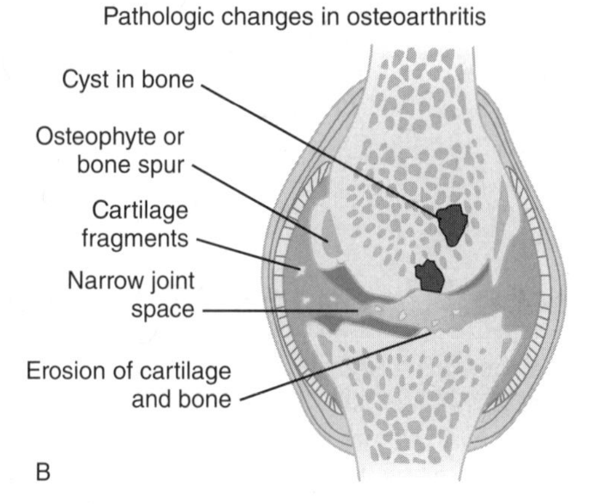

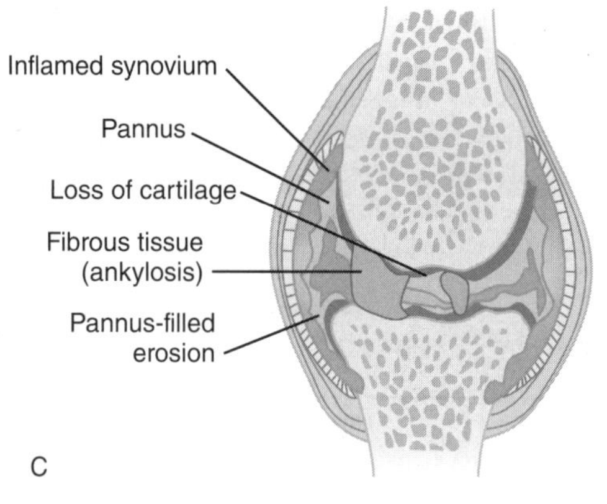

Figure 11.1 (Continued) Joint changes.

by the adjoining tendons (see **Figure 11.2**). Adolescents are particularly vulnerable to Osgood-Schlatter during the growth spurts throughout puberty, when muscles, tendons, and bones may be growing at variable rates. In addition, enhanced rates of pulling on the growth plate may occur with the repetitive movements often found in sport, such as running and jumping. Osgood-Schlatter may be viewed as an overuse or repetitive stress injury from the repetitive movements.

Sever's disease is another bone growth issue that can arise in children and adolescents. Unlike below the knee as in Osgood-Schlatter disease, Sever's impacts the heel (see **Figure 11.3**). This disease typically develops during a growth spurt in puberty. During these spurts, bones, tendons, and muscles may grow at variable rates, causing "pulling" in various locations, including on the growth plate in the heel. Activities involving running and jumping can further pull on this growth plate, resulting in a swelling and subsequent irritation with the growth plate in the heel. Key symptoms include:

- Redness or swelling in the heel
- Stiffness in the heels and feet in the morning
- Pain when squeezing the heel

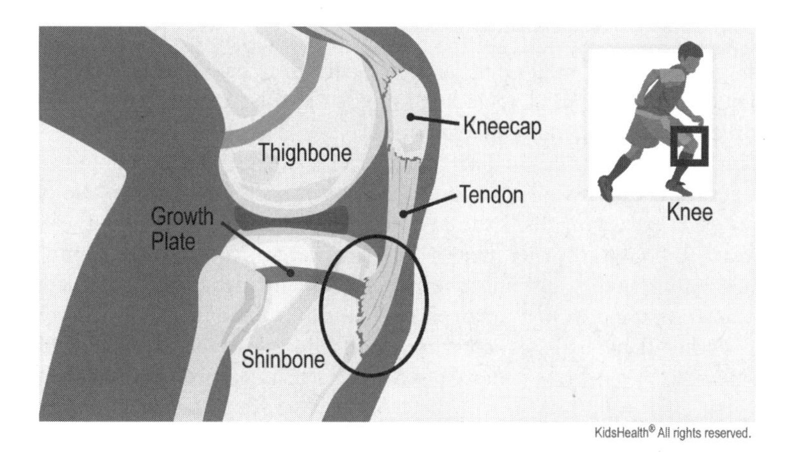

Figure 11.2 Osgood-Schlatter disease.

Reproduced from Su, A. (2019a, January). *Osgood-Schlatter disease.* https://kidshealth.org/en/parents/osgood.html

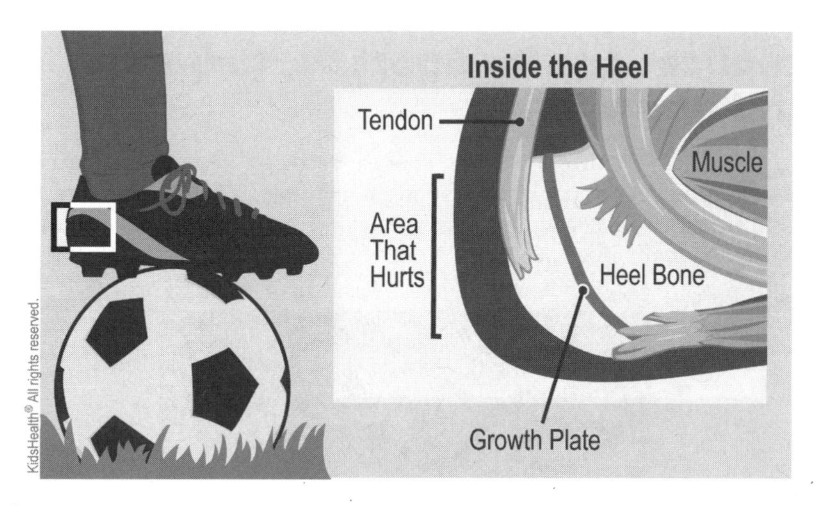

Figure 11.3 Sever's disease.

Reproduced from Su, A. (2019b, January). *Sever's disease.* https://kidshealth.org/en/parents/severs-disease.html

Once developed, Osgood-Schlatter and Sever's disease would cause considerable pain for the developing athletes and inhibit their ability to participate without pain.

How Arthritis, Osgood-Schlatter, and Sever's Disease Are Recognized

In children and adolescents under 16 years of age, *juvenile idiopathic arthritis* (a kind of rheumatoid arthritis) is the most common form of arthritis. In addition to the core symptoms mentioned above, individuals with juvenile arthritis may also experience fever, rashes, or swollen lymph nodes. It can also negatively impact their growth.

Arthritis can be diagnosed via a medical exam. The doctor may look for swelling and range of motion and possibly perform a blood test. Some imaging techniques can also be used, including x-rays and MRIs, to get a better glimpse of internal swelling or deterioration of cartilage.

Similarly, for Osgood-Schlatter and Sever's, doctors may examine for redness, tenderness, and swelling around the knee or heel. An x-ray can also offer a glimpse of internal growths. Externally for Osgood-Schlatter disease, there may be a painful, bony protrusion below the knee and at the top of the shin. Given the link with growth spurts in puberty, Osgood-Schlatter is often diagnosed in adolescence, and more often in boys. When it is diagnosed in females, it typically occurs earlier than in males, considering that females typically enter puberty (and growth spurts) first. It most often occurs in one knee at a time but can be experienced in both simultaneously. Similarly, Sever's disease is more often reported during adolescence and for those active in athletics. Given their association with the growth spurt, Osgood-Schlatter and Sever's disease typically go away when bones stop growing as actively, approximately when adolescents are 14 to 18 years old.

Implications for Sport Participation and Performance

Physical activity is one of the better nonpharmacologic treatments for arthritis. It can keep adjoining muscle tissue strong and flexible. It can also decrease bone loss (particularly in older individuals) and replenish the lubricating chemicals in and around joints. Together, physical activity can help manage pain. However,

for individuals with arthritis, starting or maintaining physical activity can also seem daunting. This may be true for young athletes who are beginning a new sport or season.

In the case of Osgood-Schlatter and Sever's disease, some of the repetitive movements such as running or jumping can enhance the likelihood of developing the disease during certain age periods. Older children and adolescents diagnosed with Osgood-Schlatter do not necessarily need to cease athletic participation. However, the pain associated with it can impact their ability to practice and perform. In some cases, the pain is severe enough where rest is warranted. In other cases, pain may be monitored, and activities curtailed to the extent necessary to support the athlete. For Sever's disease, the athlete may also need to cut down or temporarily eliminate the activities that cause the most pain. Non–weight-bearing activities (e.g,, swimming, stretching, strengthening exercises) may be beneficial. Once pain subsides, athletes can typically return to all activities at full capacity.

Coaching Techniques and Strategies

While the physical activity (e.g., stretching, warm-ups, practice) can have benefits for pain management, coaches should monitor the pain being reported and experienced for athletes with arthritis, Osgood-Schlatter, or Sever's. Where applicable, the support of athletic trainers should be enlisted to help prevent and treat pain. There are a variety of pain-reducing pharmacologic treatments for arthritis (coverage of which is beyond the scope of this book). There are also some interventions (e.g., massage, physical therapy) and lifestyle factors, such as diet, as well as hot and/or cold treatments.

Heat therapy can promote blood flow and circulation to ease pain. Heat may come in the form of hot showers, compresses, or heat packs. At other times, cold therapy can be useful to reduce swelling. This could be with ice bags or baths, cold

packs, a bag of frozen vegetables, or an "ice massage" in which ice is applied directly to the joint. One way to do this is to freeze water in small paper cups, then peel away the top portion to expose the ice as you massage. Coaches can know what an athlete prefers and take steps along with athletic trainers and others to make therapies available. Athletic trainers may suggest the Rest, Ice, Compression, Elevation (RICE) method for treatment. However, refer the athlete to an athletic trainer, physical therapist, doctor, or other medical professional for diagnosis and treatment.

There are some other behavioral techniques that can help manage arthritic pain:

- Stretching before and after practice and competition
- Meditation
- Deep breathing
- Guided imagery
- Progressive relaxation
- Yoga

Other ideas are more specific to Osgood-Schlatter or Sever's disease. For instance, according to Nemours Health, youth athletes with Osgood-Schlatter or Sever's disease may benefit from:

- Wearing shock-absorbing insoles in shoes, including cleats
- Avoid heavy and high-heeled shoes (Sever's)
- Heating the area (hot pack, warm cloth) prior to practice or competition
- Icing the area after practice or competition (Su, 2019a; Su, 2019b)
- Wearing protective kneepads (Osgood-Schlatter)

In addition to these ideas, coaches can explore with athletes and medical professionals if there are supports or braces that might make movement easier and pain more tolerable. Coaches can create an open, collaborative dialogue where athletes know they can talk about their pain experiences and needs as well as voice their opinions. Their opinions can help guide old or new methods aimed at reducing pain, as well as let the coach know when to curtail activities to help reduce pain.

VIGNETTE Part Two

"Coach. A quick word?" Coach Reuben Gonzalez turned to see Robert Yonder approaching him with his son Jensen. He loved it when players arrived early and not just on time.

"Hi Robert. Hi Jensen." Gonzalez smiled at both.

"Hey Coach," said Robert. "I wanted to let you know that Jensen's right knee has been bothering him. He's been limping around the house for the last few days and icing it and stuff."

"Ah, I'm sorry to hear that. What seems to be the problem Jensen?"

Jensen shuffled uncomfortably.

"It's alright son. Just tell him the truth."

"Well, Coach. My knee has been feeling really sore when we do sprints during warmups or when I have to chase a ball." Jensen was almost whispering.

"I see. Okay, I'm sorry to hear that. What do you think is causing it?"

Reuben interrupted. "Well, Sarah thinks it's his shoes. He changed shoes about a month ago. They grow so fast you know!"

"Okay, well that's definitely a possibility," Gonzalez continued. "But what do you think it is, Jensen?"

"I don't know Coach. I just know it hurts when I practice and play. Whenever I do something explosive like sprinting or jumping or lunging it really hurts and makes it worse."

Jensen was visibly upset, and Gonzalez knew he was thinking about potentially missing practices and games.

"Okay, I'll tell you what. I know this is hard for you, but I appreciate you being honest and telling me. I don't know what it is either, so Robert, I'd like you to get it checked out with a doctor before Jensen continues playing. It could be nothing, but I want to be sure in case we are making it worse."

Robert nodded.

"So, Jensen. Listen, I know this isn't what you wanted to hear, but how about being one of my assistants this evening and helping me out instead? You don't have to, of course, but it would be a great way to still be with the team tonight and learn what we're doing?"

This time it was Jensen who looked for approval from his dad and then nodded.

"Okay, let's get to practice then. See you later, Robert, and let me know as soon as you know. Jensen's a valuable member of our team and we want him playing baseball for a long time to come!"

Additional Resources

- Arthritis Foundation: https://www.arthritis.org
- Mayo Clinic: https://www.mayoclinic.org/diseases-conditions/osgood-schlatter-disease/symptoms-causes/syc-20354864
- Arthritis Foundation: https://www.arthritis.org/health-wellness/treatment/complementary-therapies/natural-therapies/mind-body-techniques-juvenile-arthritis

Summary

- Arthritis is related to swelling, tenderness, or pain in one or more joints. The most common forms of arthritis are osteoarthritis and rheumatoid arthritis.
  - *Osteoarthritis* occurs when cartilage (rubbery, connective tissue between joints) breaks down over time.
  - *Rheumatoid arthritis* is when the immune system attacks the body's own tissue, including joints.
- Osgood-Schlatter disease involves pain and swelling below the kneecap. Internally, the growth plate above the shin is pulled on by the adjoining tendons.
- Sever's disease involves pain and swelling in the heel, as the growth plate is pulled during growth spurts. Repetitive movements such as running or jumping

can enhance the likelihood of developing Osgood-Schlatter or Sever's disease in some athletes.

- Children and adolescents diagnosed with arthritis, Osgood-Schlatter, or Sever's do not necessarily need to cease all athletic participation.
- The pain associated with these conditions can impact their ability to practice and perform.
- Rest periods may be necessary.
- Coaches can know the extent of the athlete's pain in relevant activities; maintain open communication with the athlete and medical professionals, including athletic trainers; and adjust physical activity as necessary.

Questions for Consideration

1. What are the similarities between Osgood-Schlatter disease and arthritis?
2. T/F: Osgood-Schlatter occurs in girls earlier than boys.
3. T/F: Physical activity is beneficial to those with arthritis.
4. If an athlete with Osgood-Schlatter wants to continue participation against the advice of medical professionals, what could you do to help them understand why the rest is important?
5. Within your sport, how could you modify your practice for an athlete with arthritis or Osgood-Schlatter disease?

References

Su, A. (2019a). *Osgood-Schlatter's disease.* https://kidshealth.org/en/parents/osgood.html
Su, A. (2019b). *Sever's disease.* https://kidshealth.org/en/parents/severs-disease.html

CHAPTER 12

Motor Disorders

VIGNETTE Part One

"Miss Cheko, Miss Cheko!" The cry crossed the gymnasium as Natalia Cheko distinguished the unmistakable whiny tone of Tobias Watts. She inwardly groaned as she turned and saw him approaching.

"Miss Cheko. Can I go to the bathroom?"

"Yes, Tobias. You may." Ten year-old Tobias shuffled on past her to the restrooms. Cheko shook her head and once again reminded herself that she, of all people, was in charge of a diverse group of 8- to 18-year-old youth learning to play pickleball. This had never been something she would have ever dreamed she'd be doing one day, but when you've got two kids who want to learn and play with other kids, and when no one else steps up to help, then Natalia Cheko must. She smiled wryly to herself and returned her focus to the kids playing on the courts.

Not but a few minutes later, "Miss Cheko" could be heard again, and again it was Tobias who approached. She sighed.

"Miss Cheko, Catherine is making fun of me," Tobias whined, not really caring whether anyone else heard. Tobias had yet to learn any sense of decorum, and it made for some awkward moments.

"Quiet down, Tobias. I'm sure she's not."

"No, she is. She is. When I serve, she copies me. It's really annoying!"

"Well, maybe she's trying to learn your great serve?"

"Nooo... she's copying me and making fun of me. I don't want to play with her."

"Come on, Tobias. I'm sure it's not like that." Cheko did her best not to roll her eyes.

"Actually," said a voice on the court to Cheko's right, "She's done something similar with me." Cheko turned to see Jasmine, one of the older players in the group, stopping play to talk. "When I hit a smash she'll do the same, even if we're not on the same court. It's a bit annoying but I didn't want to say anything."

"Seeeeee?" said Tobias, far too loudly. The conversation was gaining the attention of all of the courts.

"Okay, okay," said Cheko quickly. "Look. Everyone go back to their games and keep going. Tobias, I'll talk with Catherine's grandma tonight when she comes to pick her up, okay? In the meantime, do you think you can let it go and just keep playing with Catherine?"

"Well, okay," responded Tobias.

"Thank you. Okay, everyone back to playing please." Cheko paused and internally sighed as play began to resume. "Why does a volunteer coach have to deal with this kind of problem?" she thought to herself. She wasn't looking forward to the conversation that had to come.

Forms, Definitions, and Prevalence

Motor disorders are broadly related to difficulties in motor skill development and capabilities, which can interfere with a variety of daily living situations, including social, academic, and play activities. There are a few more common motor disorders recognized in the Diagnostic and Statistical Manual, including *developmental coordination disorder* and *tic disorders*. For tic disorders, there is Tourette's disorder, persistent motor or vocal tic disorder, and provisional tic disorder (American Psychiatric Association, 2013). Following is more specific information about each type.

- **Developmental coordination disorder** involves difficulties in developing and executing motor skills. Children with this disorder may often be described as clumsy and may be inaccurate and slow with movements.
- **Tic disorders** involve movements (or sounds) as well, but in the form of "tics" or sudden, rapid, and recurrent movements or vocalizations. Tourette's syndrome—where both multiple motor and/or more vocal tics are presents—is one of the tic disorders.

The prevalence of developmental coordination disorder is about 5 to 6% of children (ages 5–11) and tic disorders about 3 to 8 per 1,000 (school age children). Many simple motor delays are common in development and may disappear over time. Also, tics may be common in childhood but may recede (American Psychiatric Association, 2013).

How Motor Disorders Are Recognized

There is typically early onset and signs of motor disorders. For developmental coordination disorder, the first signs may be related to delays in motor milestones (e.g., walking). Thereafter, difficulty may be observed in other motor tasks, such as assembling puzzles, handwriting, and sport play.

For tic disorders, the tics tend to first appear at between 4 and 6 years, may peak in late childhood/early adolescence, and decline through adolescence and beyond. The "disorder" is only diagnosed if the issues begin to interfere significantly with participation in and performance of daily activities, including at home, school, and social and community settings.

The tics can be simple, involving one muscle group (e.g., head twitching, nose wrinkling, blinking, lip biting, grimacing) or complex involving multiple muscle groups. Complex tics may include jumping, kicking, or mimicking others' movements. These tics may be misunderstood as being done "on purpose." Tics can also be vocal; still being simple (coughing, grunting) or complex (saying or yelling words or phrases).

Implications for Sport Participation and Performance

Delayed motor development and performance, and seemingly purposeless and/or involuntary movements, have implications for sport performance. In cases of developmental coordination disorder, the individuals may lag behind peers in expected performance of motor skills and tasks. It may be challenging for them to "keep up" with their peers in games and play, whether unorganized or organized. The presence of developmental coordination disorder may impact sport and activity choice, as they opt for activities, sports, or positions involving less fine motor movements. For tic disorders, the motor movements may interfere with fluid motor movements and performance. The tics may seem to interfere with circumstances in sport in which there are typically moments of calm and stillness, such as prior to a tee shot in golf, a snap in football, a pitch in baseball, or a dive into the pool. The level of potential interference may depend upon whether the tics are isolated to one smaller muscle group or are more complex tics involving multiple muscle groups. Tics can be impacted by perceived stress, so a high pressure game situation may prompt tics (in terms of intensity or frequency) that are not apparent in lower pressure and stress circumstances such as practice.

Coaching Techniques and Strategies

Coaches may need to exhibit patience with individuals with developmental coordination disorder in mastering tasks. Some research has indicated ways to help individuals with developmental coordination disorder. For instance, task-oriented approaches to motor learning appear promising (Jane et al., 2018). These approaches focus on spending time developing the specific skills with which individual athletes appear to be struggling. Coaches should also carefully monitor feedback to develop the athlete's physical and athletic sense of competence (Noordstar et al., 2017). Along those lines, coaches may:

- Set specific goals for motor tasks.
- Offer specific feedback that is simple and goal-related.
- Emphasize correct movement and execution (over incorrect ones).
- Find or encourage extra time to work on tasks with the athlete.
- Monitor and record progress and show the athlete improvements.

Tics can be "temperamental" or impacted by the stress in the environment. They can be worsened by stressful or exhausting tasks and situations, and individuals may have fewer tics when engaging in calm, focused tasks. If it is evident that some tasks seem to elicit more stress than others, coaches can have an array of more focused, calmer alternatives spread throughout the day or week. Individuals with tics may have a level of anxiety of being in social situations (including team settings). To help minimize this, coaches may consider:

- Informing and educating teammates about tics (with the athlete's permission).
- Model "not focusing" on the tic(s). When they occur, just continue.

Sometimes, individuals with tic disorders may involuntarily mimic others by making sounds or gestures. Often, these mimicked sounds or movements are misinterpreted as intentional by others, including teachers and coaches. Understanding and knowing this possibility can help coaches and others from taking things personally and reacting negatively.

VIGNETTE Part Two

Natalia Cheko started shutting down the pickleball activity a few minutes before 8 PM. She asked several of the youth to help her pick up and put away the equipment, and family members began filtering into the gymnasium to pick up their kids. Natalia kept an eye out for Catherine's grandmother, who she spotted at the side of the gym.

"Mrs. Lambert. Can I have a quick word?" She quickly walked over. She wasn't looking forward to the conversation, but it had to happen.

"Hi, Mrs. Lambert. How are you?"

"I'm well, thank you. And you?"

"Good. I'm good. I just wanted to have a quick word with you about something Catherine has been doing. I didn't know if there was something going on, but some of the kids have commented that she seems to copy their movements, and it's been bothering them a little. Have you noticed anything like that?"

"Oh, yes, of course. She has a tic disorder. It was diagnosed a couple of years ago. She can't help it."

"A tic disorder?"

"Yes, and part of it is that she mimics motions, and most times she doesn't even know it. I'm sorry. I should have told you about it."

"Okay, well thanks for telling me now. Is this something I can tell the other kids in the program? I don't think they understand, and it would help."

"Oh yes, of course. And, I don't think Catherine would mind sharing about it either. Catherine!"

Catherine ran over from where she was talking with a friend.

"Catherine," her grandma said. "Coach Cheko didn't know about your tic disorder. Next time you have pickleball, can you share with the group about it so they know?"

"Sure, grandma." Catherine said happily.

"Thank you both very much," said Cheko relieved and said her goodbyes as Catherine and her grandma headed out the door.

"Sometimes," she thought to herself, "You have to do the hard thing to make it easier. And, I wish I'd thought of doing some kind of health history questionnaire before we began. This problem would have never been a problem! This coaching thing is harder than I thought."

Additional Resources

- Tourette Association of America: https://tourette.org/
- Understood: https://www.understood.org/en/learning-thinking-differences/child-learning-disabilities/dyspraxia/understanding-developmental-coordination-disorder-dcd

Summary

- Motor disorders are broadly related to challenges in motor skill development and capabilities that can interfere with a variety of daily living situations, including social, academic, and play activities.
- The prevalence of developmental coordination disorder is approximately 5 to 6% of children (ages 5–11).
- The prevalence of tic disorders is about 3 to 8 per 1,000 (school age children).
- The disrupted motor movements can interfere with athletic development and play.
- Coaches can understand symptoms of motor disorders and engage in a variety of behavioral techniques to facilitate development of these athletes.

Questions for Consideration

1. What are the differences between a developmental coordination disorder and tic disorder?

2. The term "fluidity" is relevant to this chapter. Why?
3. Give five examples of tics.
4. It is important to emphasize ___________ movement and execution.
5. Which strategies should you use to coach an individual with a motor disorder?

References

American Psychiatric Association. (2013). Motor disorders. In *Diagnostic and statistical manual of mental disorders* (5th ed.).

Jane, J. Y., Burnett, A. F., & Sit, C. H. (2018). Motor skill interventions in children with developmental coordination disorder: A systematic review and meta-analysis. *Archives of Physical Medicine and Rehabilitation*, *99*(10), 2076-2099.

Noordstar, J. J., van der Net, J., Voerman, L., Helders, P. J., & Jongmans, M. J. (2017). The effect of an integrated perceived competence and motor intervention in children with developmental coordination disorder. *Research in Developmental Disabilities*, *60*, 162–175. https://doi.org/10.1016/j.ridd.2016.12.002

PART 5

Physical and Mental Health

CHAPTER 13

Athlete Triad

VIGNETTE Part One

The rhythmic whirring sound of an erg was the first thing Coach Andrew ("Andy") Patterson heard as he walked into the boathouse. The sky was dark outside, but someone was getting an early start. He dropped his laptop off in his cramped office and walked into the erg room. If he had guessed, he would have put his money on Lisa Buchanan, and he was not disappointed. Even at an open weight training camp, there was a lot at stake for these athletes who had dedicated their lives to representing their country. And, so it seemed, Lisa was intent on making sure she made it.

"Early start for you, Lisa," said Patterson as he approached.

"Hey, Coach," responded Lisa between breaths. "Just trying to work out some stuff."

"Okay, well don't do too much. We've a busy day of practice ahead."

"I won't. I'll be done soon."

Patterson turned and headed back to his office smiling to himself. "If only all of his athletes had that same internal desire to be their absolute best. True, you didn't get to camp without being an amazing talent, but there is always that little something that differentiates the best from the very good.

Practice went well that day, but Patterson was surprised to see Lisa once again hitting the erg early the next morning before others had arrived.

"Lisa? More training?" Patterson asked with a raised eyebrow.

"Yeah, Coach. I messed some stuff up yesterday and spent a lot of time doing technique stuff. I didn't feel like I got my full workout in."

"Hmmm... okay. Well, listen. I know you know your own body well and I trust your judgment, but our training plan works. Don't overdo it, okay? Sleep is important too!"

"Got it Coach."

"The weekend's coming, so take a day off to rest your body and recharge."

Yesterday, Patterson had put it down to commitment. But commitment could go too far. In fact, Lisa's numbers on the water hadn't been great yesterday. It could have been down to who she'd been partnered with in the pairs, but maybe not as well. He made a mental note to check with his assistant coach, Rebecca French, to see if she'd noticed anything. His athletes were adults who knew their bodies, and while his training program was clear, he recognized that there needed to be flexibility and differentiation for each athlete. But, he sure didn't want his athletes overtraining.

Forms, Definitions, and Prevalence

The athlete triad is a syndrome consisting of three core, interrelated conditions, including energy deficiency, menstrual dysfunction, and reduced bone health (including osteoporosis). Reduced energy (or caloric) deficiency may be the factor that underlies the triad. There is an imbalance between calories burned and consumed, with athletes not taking in enough calories to support their physical activity needs (see **Figure 13.1**). Essentially, they are underfueling themselves. Often, this caloric imbalance occurs due to intentional food restrictions and a desire to be lean. In some cases, disordered eating is apparent, and in more extreme cases, it may lead to eating disorders, including anorexia and bulimia.

Another aspect of the triad is menstrual dysfunction, with the most extreme cases involving amenorrhea, or the absence of a menstrual cycle for 3 or more months. Individuals with the triad also have a higher risk of weakened bone structure and health, which may result in osteoporosis (see **Figure 13.2**), as well as bone and stress fractures.

While the triad traditionally has been observed in female athletes, the *Female and Male Athlete Triad Coalition* also allows room for the triad in male athletes. For male athletes, they may experience the same energy deficiency and reduced bone health, although they would experience other types of reproductive suppression, such as reduced testosterone levels. The symptoms associated with the triad exist on a continuum of severity. While prevalence data ranges widely, anywhere from 16 to 60% of female athletes report at least one symptom of the triad. Medical attention should be sought when one of the symptoms appears, not only when all three are apparent.

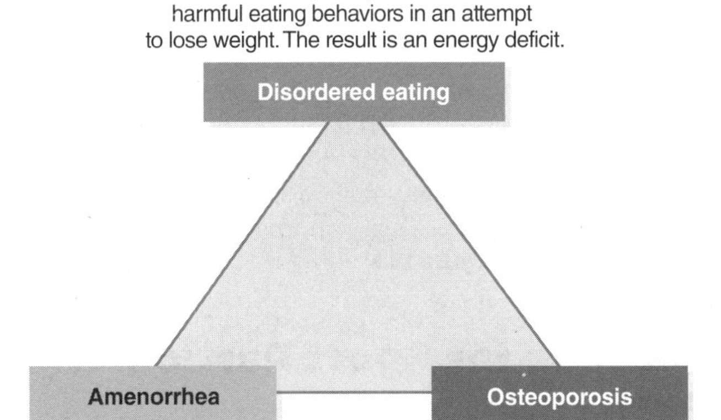

Figure 13.1 The female athlete triad.

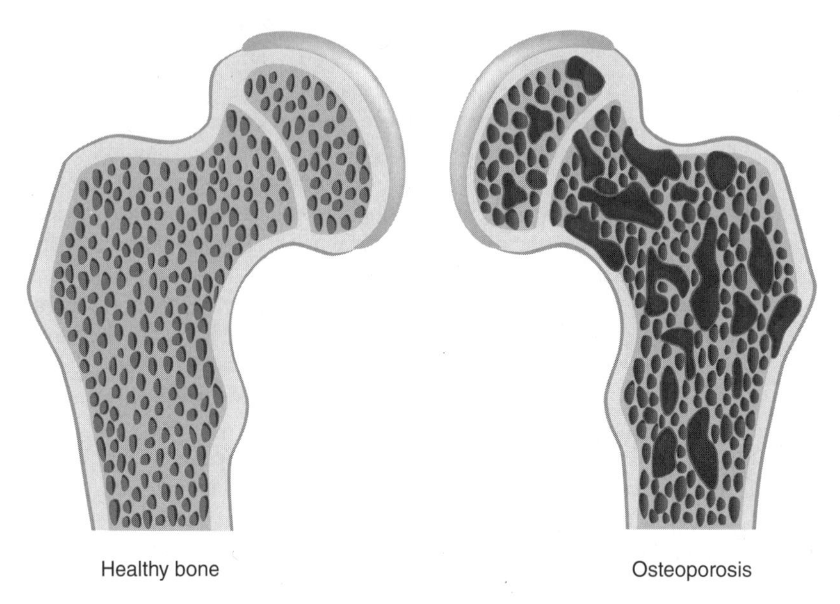

Figure 13.2 Osteoporosis.

How the Athlete Triad Is Recognized

There are a variety of risk factors for the athlete triad. Given that energy deficiency is a primary cause of the triad, many of the risk factors relate to a desire to be lean, including skipping meals, dissatisfaction with one's body, perfectionistic habits, and the belief that weight will negatively impact performance.

Some of these factors may be enhanced with sports that seem to favor leanness (e.g., gymnastics, figure skating, cross country) and those that require uniforms that are more revealing (e.g., cross country uniforms, swimwear, volleyball uniforms). Sports that factor in weight classes (e.g., wrestling, rowing) may also enhance an athlete's drive to be thin (see **Figure 13.3**).

Implications for Sport Participation and Performance

Some of the signs and symptoms of the triad have direct implications for physical activity and sport participation for female and male athletes. For instance, the energy deficits may translate into reduced energy and workload capabilities. There may be noticeable weight loss and a seemingly obsessive or compulsive need to engage in physical activity, even above and beyond what the coach requires of their team during regularly scheduled practices. The negative impact upon bone health may increase the rates of stress fractures and injuries.

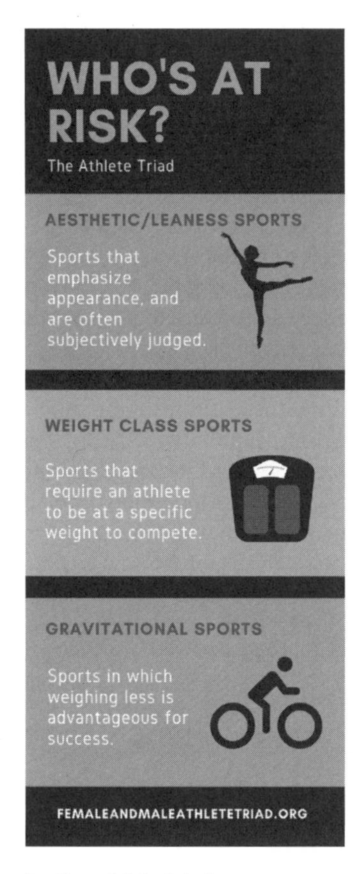

Figure 13.3 Risk factors for the athlete triad.

Courtesy of The Female and Male Athlete Triad Coalition.

Coaching Techniques and Strategies

Nutrition and energy imbalance are a primary cause of the triad. Therefore, coaches can create a team environment that is positive and person oriented (which emphasize health and development over performance) and emphasizes modifiable factors such as practice, effort, and personal improvement as it relates to performance over body shape and size. Along those lines, coaches should be cognizant of the explicit messages they (or other athletes) may verbalize about body shape, size, or comparison. Even those done "in jest" can be troublesome. They can also remind athletes that sport participation is supposed to be enjoyable and fun.

Coaches should promote and discuss realistic goals that emphasize personal improvement, which can lessen the likelihood of frustration and stress. Coaches should be flexible and adaptable in practice schedules and not demonstrate rigidity to routines. Moreover, coaches can explicitly discuss with their entire team—also to not single out athletes—the importance of proper nutrition for fueling and performance. If available, nutritionists or health educators could give guest talks to the team. Together, coaches can help encourage a balance of sport with other interests, and that their sport involvement is a part of a healthy, lifelong lifestyle of exercise and physical activity, which has physical, mental, spiritual, and social benefits.

One or more of the triad conditions may require referral and medical attention. So, above and beyond coaching "techniques" relevant for the athletes, coaches should be able to recognize signs and symptoms, reach out to athletes, and refer to the appropriate medical and mental health professionals. The National Eating Disorder Association (NEDA) offers a useful toolkit (see additional resources) for coaches to further recognize signs of energy deficiency and how to reach out to athletes of concern and to communicate with athletes about health. An athlete does not need to meet the criteria for an *eating disorder* (e.g., anorexia, bulimia) for dietary habits to be problematic. Rather, *disordered eating*, still involves food and calorie restriction or avoidance to the extent that athletes do not take in enough calories needed to support daily routines and sport activity. Early identification and intervention with disordered eating and eating disorders can be very important in terms of recovery. Additionally, it is important for coaches to know that eating patterns (including problematic ones) can be pervasive on teams, with teammates trying the same if they perceive it is beneficial in terms of performance or aesthetically. There may be particular risk in sports such as gymnastics, dance, figure skating, diving, cross country, or track and field. According to the NEDA (2013) toolkit, some signs and symptoms of problematic energy restriction and loss include:

- Decreased concentration and focus
- Increased fatigue and amount of time needed between workouts and competitions to recover
- Higher rates or intensity of injuries
- Heightened sensitivity to cold temperatures
- Light-headedness and dizziness
- Abdominal pains
- More negative social interactions or withdrawal for teammates
- Signs of perfectionism
- Ritualistic around food intake
- Excessive concerns with body weight
- Enhanced or prolonged "extra" workouts (perhaps on their own)
- Teammate reports of concern

An athlete may attempt to hide behaviors (e.g., eating or working out privately) or weight loss (e.g., wearing longer, loose fitting clothing). Coaches do not want to confront an athlete with whom they have concerns in a public, demeaning, or potentially embarrassing way. This may prompt the athlete(s) to go into more "hiding." Rather, if there are concerns, a coach should consider gentle ways to approach an athlete but still be as direct and straightforward as possible, citing their concerns. The NEDA encourages involving parents and guardians in the discussion. However, if there is a problem, the athlete may not have disclosed it to their parents or guardians yet. Therefore, the coach may be able to encourage and help the athlete to do so. In many cases, medical attention may be necessary, and there may be an urgency to act quickly. A coach's open and supportive communication may be very important to encourage disclosure to parents, guardians, and medical professionals. Coaches can also facilitate adherence to interventions. The NEDA toolkit contains sample conversations that coaches may have with athletes about their observations and concerns. Chapter 16 of this book (Mental Health and Sleep) has more information on how coaches can make referrals in such situations and consider confidentiality for the athlete at the same time.

VIGNETTE Part Two

Later that morning, Coach Patterson had a brief meeting with his assistant coach, Rebecca French. Rebecca had a more personal relationship with the rowers, not necessarily because she was female and he was not, but it didn't hurt. Plus, because he ultimately made the hard decisions on who made the team and who didn't, the rowers were a little more cautious to reveal all around him.

"What are your thoughts on Lisa?" he asked Rebecca.

"What do you mean? I mean, she's always given everything."

"I know, I know. But the last couple of mornings, she's been here before me on the erg."

"Really? That's interesting."

"Why do you say that?"

"Well, I'd come in on Sunday to work on my Master's classes and she was here rowing then. I didn't think much of it, but on reflection, she was here quite a while getting extra work in. It sounds like she's doing a lot on her own."

"Interesting. Have you noticed anything else that might suggest something is going on? I don't want anyone overtraining."

"Well, her times haven't been great recently, which doesn't always mean anything as you know, but they're not as good as they normally are. But..."

"What?"

"Well, it's probably nothing, but..."

"But what?"

"Doesn't she seem thinner to you?"

Patterson paused to think about it.

"You know," he said softly, "I think you could be right. We're around them so much that we don't notice little changes, but I bet you're right. She does look thinner." A look of concern crossed his face. "But losing a bit of weight doesn't necessarily mean anything as fitness levels improve."

"The signs are there, Andy. The excessive exercise, the weight loss, the decrease in performances. There could be an underlying issue that's serious." Rebecca also looked worried.

"Okay, I think you're right. Neither of us is qualified to help Lisa if she does have a serious problem. I think it's time we went up the chain to find out how we can best help her."

"Agreed."

"Let's not discuss this with Lisa for now and I'll contact the national headquarters to see what policies and procedures we need to follow."

This wasn't going to be an easy process, and Patterson had never had to help someone with what sounded like an eating disorder of some kind. But the care and well-being of his athletes superseded anything else; that much he knew. So, while Rebecca went to start practice, he picked up the phone and started dialing.

Additional Resources

- The Female and Male Athlete Triad Coalition: https://www.femaleandmaleathlete triad.org
- NEDA: Coach and Athletic Trainer Toolkit: https://www.nationaleatingdisorders .org/sites/default/files/nedaw18/3.%20CoachandTrainerToolkit%20-%20Copy .pdf
- National Eating Disorder Association (NEDA): https://www.nationaleatingdisorders .org/
- NCAA: https://www.ncaa.org/sites/default/files/Female%20Athlete%20Triad.pdf
- NCAA Coaches Handbook: Managing the Athlete Triad: https://athletewellness .uncg.edu/wp-content/uploads/2014/05/Coaches-Handbook.pdf

Summary

- The athlete triad is a syndrome consisting of three core, interrelated conditions, including energy deficiency, menstrual dysfunction, and reduced bone health.
- While the triad traditionally has been observed in female athletes, the triad is also observed in male athletes. For male athletes, they may experience the same energy deficiency and reduced bone health, although they would experience other types of reproductive suppression, such as reduced testosterone levels.
- The symptoms associated with the triad exist on a continuum of severity. While prevalence data ranges widely, anywhere from 16 to 60% of female athletes report at least one symptom of the triad.
- Coaches can create a team environment that is positive and person-oriented (which emphasize health and development over performance) and which emphasizes modifiable factors such as practice, effort, and personal improvement as it relates to performance over body shape and size.
- One or more of the triad conditions may require referral and medical attention. Signs and symptoms of energy restriction and loss include:
  - Decreased concentration and focus
  - Increased fatigue and amount of time needed between workouts and competitions to recover
  - Higher rates or intensity of injuries
  - Heightened sensitivity to cold temperatures
  - Light-headedness and dizziness
  - Abdominal pains
  - More negative social interactions or withdrawal for teammates, signs of perfectionism
  - Ritualistic around food intake
  - Excessive concerns with body weight
  - Enhanced or prolonged "extra" workouts (perhaps on their own)
  - Teammate reports of concern
- If concerned, a coach should:
  - Be gentle, but direct and straightforward as possible, citing their concerns.
  - Involve parents and guardians in the discussion.
    - However, if there is a problem, the athlete may not have disclosed to his or her parents or guardians yet. Therefore, the coach may be able to encourage and help the athlete to do so.

- Medical attention may be necessary.
- A coach's open and supportive communication may be very important to encourage disclosure to parents, guardians, and medical professionals.

Questions for Consideration

1. Explain the female athlete triad and why it is a problem for athletes.
2. T/F: The condition is a female-only condition.
3. What are three signs and symptoms that your athlete might have the athlete triad?
4. Some athletes will continue to deliberately lose weight because weight loss has led to increased performances. What steps can you take as coach to combat this argument?
5. What are the differences between an eating disorder and disordered eating?

References

Findlay, R. J., Macrae, E. H., Whyte, I. Y., Easton, C., & Forrest, L. J. (2020). How the menstrual cycle and menstruation affect sporting performance: Experiences and perceptions of elite female rugby players. *British Journal of Sports Medicine, 54*(18), 1108–1113.

National Eating Disorders Association. (2013). *Coach and athletic trainer toolkit*. Author. https://www.nationaleatingdisorders.org/sites/default/files/nedaw18/3.%20CoachandTrainer Toolkit%20-%20Copy.pdf

CHAPTER 14

Diabetes

VIGNETTE Part One

"Props, get your feet set!" Coach Linda McMillan shouted across the field to her forwards. It was the little things that could make a difference once the scrum engaged and pushed, but she also didn't want it to collapse either. There were few things worse than a referee blowing for a penalty because her scrum didn't engage or set up properly.

"Okay, reset. Reset. Let's try that again." Practice wasn't going according to plan, but that's why it was called practice. She tried to be patient and watched carefully, as this time her props did get their feet set and ready for the crouch, bind, and set process of a proper scrum.

"Good. Good. Okay, let's get some fitness work in to round out practice." She let her fitness coach, Veronica Gates, take over the session as she watched. Her team wasn't ready for the upcoming World Cup, but they were making steady progress, and she knew they had every chance of getting out of pool play.

Fitness was a relative term in rugby, given the vast differences in physiques of the positions played, but she wanted all of her players fit to last the full 80 minutes, so she watched as her players were put through their paces. Her props, Beth Denden and her team captain, Ashely Porgue, were the largest players on her team, and it was hard for them especially, but McMillan didn't want to lose because only some of her team was fit.

Ashley, in particular, had been a concern for McMillan. At a very solid 225 lbs, she could move a wall, but struggled of late to last the full 80 minutes. This had become a concern in practices too, and McMillan could see Ashley dragging almost to a standstill, hands on hips and breathing hard. She didn't like what she saw, especially given her integral part of the team's balance. Maybe it was time for a talk.

Forms, Definitions, and Prevalence

Diabetes is a disease related to when blood glucose (or blood sugar) is too high. Glucose is derived from food and is a source of energy. A hormone called insulin (produced in the pancreas) is responsible for breaking down the glucose and making it available to the cells in the body for energy purposes. However, sometimes glucose is not broken down in the way that it should be for effective use. It is possible that the body does not produce insulin at all, does not produce enough

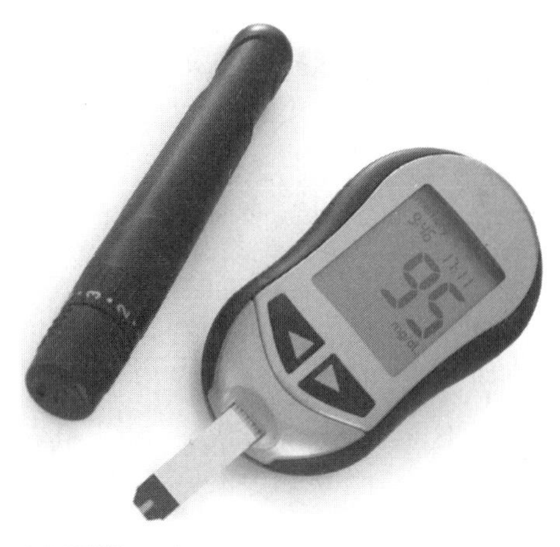

© CANARYLUC/Shutterstock.

insulin, or it is not working effectively. When this occurs, the blood glucose stays in the blood stream and does not reach the cells. The excess blood sugar is a defining characteristic of diabetes. There are two primary forms of diabetes: type 1 and type 2 (there are also some other forms, including gestational diabetes). In type 1, insulin is not produced. In fact, the immune system attacks the pancreatic cells that produce insulin. Those with type 1 diabetes need to take insulin daily. Type 2 diabetes, on the other hand, develops over time. The excess blood sugar associated with both types can cause serious health problems, including heart disease, stroke, kidney disease, nerve damage, eye and dental problems, and foot problems.

According to the American Diabetes Association (ADA), approximately 10.5% of the population in the United States has some form of diabetes, with type 2 being more common than type 1. The prevalence of diabetes in youth is lower, with the ADA reporting about 210,000 individuals under the age of 20 having been diagnosed with diabetes (approximately 0.25% of those of that age). It is estimated that 1.5 million Americans are diagnosed with diabetes each year, and there are millions of undiagnosed cases.

Different individuals may have various blood sugar target levels. Low blood sugar is known as hypoglycemia and can be serious. Initially, the body may react to low blood sugar by releasing epinephrine. Over time, if levels continue to drop, the brain and bodily systems may stop functioning as they should. People may have different reactions to low blood sugar, such as shakiness, anxiety, sweating or chills, confusion, increased heart rate, dizziness, nausea, tingling, headaches, and seizures.

How Diabetes Is Recognized

Type 1 diabetes is typically diagnosed in childhood or young adulthood. Type 2 diabetes, which is more common (approximately 90% of patients), is more typically diagnosed in middle or late adulthood. Type 2 tends to develop slowly over the course of years, and symptoms may be mild and unnoticeable up until when one or more serious health issue(s) arises. Some of these symptoms include increased thirst and urination, increased hunger, fatigue, blurred vision, numbness of feet or hands, slow healing of sores, and unexplained weight loss.

Implications for Sport Participation and Performance

Athletes with diabetes may be found at all levels of sport, from youth to recreational, up to competitive elite and Olympic athletes. Broadly, the symptoms associated with diabetes could certainly be linked with physical activity and sport (e.g., fatigue, blurred vision, numbness of feet or hands, slow healing, and unexplained weight loss). Athletes with diabetes may participate with some level of apprehension or anxiety related to medical issues that could arise during practice or competition (e.g., hypoglycemia).

Sports such as baseball or softball may be ideal for athletes with diabetes as they tend to require shorter bursts of physical activity, and the "breaks" in the dugout in between half-innings and innings, athletes may more formally monitor blood glucose and regulate as necessary. In other sports, such as distance running or other endurance events (e.g., triathlons), athletes may need to carefully manage fuel sources (Harris & White, 2012). Athletes may need to consider how they are able to wear external devices such as insulin pumps in certain sports (e.g., wrestling, football).

Considering that a general lack of physical activity and excess weight are risk factors for developing type 2 diabetes, the physical activity inherent in sport (especially if it translates into part of a long-term lifestyle) can be a protective factor in managing diabetes. However, there are risks associated with physical activity for the athlete with diabetes, including exercise-induced hypoglycemia (the body's blood sugar/glucose is lower than normal levels) and ketosis (the body burns fat instead because there is a lack of carbohydrates available). Athletes with diabetes may participate for the protective benefits that the physical activity component offers but may also exercise certain precautions.

Coaching Techniques and Strategies

Coaches should be able to recognize when one or more symptoms may be indicative of diabetes in an athlete. An athlete's well-being is of paramount importance, and medical support should be sought. Coaches are not typically trained or qualified to support an athlete with diabetes; it is important to work with a medical professional and support the athlete in a way that places their needs first. Some research suggests considerations for athletes with diabetes (e.g., Harris & White, 2012; Hornsby & Chetlin, 2005; Horton & Subauste, 2016). While these studies investigated competitive athletes, most of the considerations apply to athletes with diabetes of all ages and across the competitive spectrum.

Medical professionals should consult with the athlete to discuss a variety of factors. These include the athlete's goals in sport, their thoughts on physical performance at varying blood glucose levels, and perceived ability to judge glucose levels without a readily available glucose meter. Medical professionals will also help inform dietary adjustments or considerations for the athlete. While helping an individual manage diabetes in the context of sport, coaches should enlist medical professional assistance. The coach needs to be part of an effective plan for participation (Draznin, 2010). For example, coaches may help supply answers to important questions such as:

- How much aerobic and anaerobic activity is required for a particular sport or position?
- How intensely will the athlete participate (e.g., frequency, duration, exertion)?
- How might blood glucose monitoring be integrated into practice and competition schedules (e.g., pre-, during, and postsession)?
- What would the risk to the athlete's self or others be if the athlete experienced a hypoglycemic episode?

As the last question indicates, (exercise-induced) hypoglycemia is a possibility for athletes with diabetes. Coaches, athletic trainers, teammates, and others should be prepared with a plan in such a scenario. A coach may communicate with the athlete about how they self-recognize low blood sugar. In addition to removal from practice or play, blood glucose levels should be checked.

Upon checking glucose levels, if it is below what is considered a "safe" target level for the athlete, some advocate for the *15-15 rule*. According to the Center for Disease Control (CDC), this rule entails having about15 grams of a fast-acting carbohydrate (e.g., a glucose tablet if available and per instructions, a sugary juice or beverage, a tablespoon of honey or syrup) and checking glucose levels again after 15 minutes. If there is no change in glucose levels after 15 minutes, the 15-gram serving may be repeated until a minimum safe target level has been reached (the reader is encouraged to talk to medical professionals and consult some of the additional resources at the end of this chapter to know more about optimal glucose ranges and associated procedures for athletes).

In severe cases, hypoglycemia may result in loss of consciousness or seizures. Emergency medical personnel should be called immediately. It should be noted that there is also a delayed hypoglycemia, in which blood sugar levels may drop several hours after physical activity (Harris & White, 2012). Knowing of this possibility, coaches can "check in" with athletes in the hours after intense workouts. Assigning the athlete a "buddy" such as a friend or teammate to stay close may also be advisable.

Coaches may also help with the extra preparations that may be necessary when traveling. A medically approved and labeled kit should be examined for completeness and may include unused syringes, blood glucose meters, test strips, alcohol swabs, insulin, insulin pump, glucagon emergency kit, and ketone testing supplies. Athletes may be encouraged to pack twice as much as they think they need. This kit should always be carried with the athlete and not in checked luggage. In addition, a current letter from a medical professional stating the athlete's needs for the supplies, active prescriptions, and a medical ID card or bracelet are also necessary (Harris & White, 2012; Horton & Subauste, 2016; MacKnight et al., 2009). Together, athletes with diabetes can participate and thrive at all levels of sport, and coaches—along with qualified medical professionals—can be a critical part of well-informed plans and pathways for athletes to be well and succeed.

VIGNETTE Part Two

Later that evening, Coach Linda McMillan closed out the team's strategy meeting and pulled Ashley to the side. She'd spoken with the team's medical staff that afternoon, but no one had reported noticing anything unusual.

"Hey, Ashley," began McMillan, "I just wanted to check in with you and see how you're doing."

"Oh, it's all good Coach, but thanks for asking."

"I'm glad to hear it. How is training going overall? Are you happy with your progress this week?"

"Uh, yeah Coach. I think so. I've gone through so many training camps, it's sort of routine for me, you know?"

"I can see that. But listen. I wanted to make sure everything was okay. I noticed you struggling a little in the fitness session at the end today." Ashley shifted her feet and McMillan noticed a look of uncertainty cross Ashley's face. She continued.

"I don't want you to be worried about your position on the team. That's not what this conversation is about, okay? I want to make sure that you're fit and healthy. We need you fit and healthy for your own health and for this team to be successful. I know you're not going to be flying like the wingers, but I was surprised you had to stop. Is there anything you're struggling with that you're willing to share with me?"

McMillan knew how much players hated admitting deficiencies and injuries to someone who selected the team, but Ashley had been part of the national team for several years, and as the captain, they had a close relationship. The next few moments would certainly test that. Ashley hesitated for a moment, and McMillan could see her weighing the options before she finally sighed, looked down, and began speaking.

"So, I'm not going to lie. I've been struggling. The last few months, I've been getting winded real easy. I don't know why. It's like I run out of gas. Sometimes, after we've run the field on a break, I feel dizzy and feel like I'm going to black out for a moment. I keep thinking it'll go away but it hasn't. It's freaking me out a bit. Nothing like this has ever happened to me."

McMillan could see how worried Ashley was and put her arm around her.

"Hey, it's going to be okay. I'm sure it's something we can figure out together and find a solution. So, let's get to the bottom of it, okay?"

Ashley nodded, still looking down. The unknown is often scarier than the truth. It was time they spoke with the national team's medical staff and found out what was going on.

Additional Resources

- American Diabetes Association (ADA): https://diabetes.org/
- National Institute of Diabetes and Digestive and Kidney Diseases (NIDDK): https://www.niddk.nih.gov/health-information/diabetes/overview/what-is-diabetes
- Center for Disease Control: https://www.cdc.gov/diabetes/basics/low-blood-sugar-treatment.html

Summary

- Diabetes is a disease related to when blood glucose (or blood sugar) is too high.
- There are two primary forms of diabetes:
    - Type 1 diabetes is typically diagnosed in childhood or young adulthood and is apparent when insulin is not produced. People with type 1 diabetes need to take insulin daily.
    - Type 2 diabetes is more common (approximately 90% of patients) and is typically diagnosed in middle or late adulthood. This form develops over time.
- Coaches should be able to recognize when one or more symptoms may be indicative of diabetes in an athlete.
- Engage in dialogue with medical professionals about the athlete's specific needs and adjust accordingly.
- Coaches can be supportive of preparations for practice, competition, and travel.
- Coaches (and teammates) can be prepared to react to an emergency, as with hypoglycemia.

Questions for Consideration

1. What is the difference between the two types of diabetes presented?
2. T/F: Type 2 diabetes is more commonly diagnosed later than type 1.
3. Which sports might be more challenging for an athlete with diabetes? Why?
4. What are exercise-induced hypoglycemia and ketosis? Why are they important terms for athletes with diabetes?
5. If an athlete informs you they have diabetes, what questions should you ask them or their parents or guardians?

References

Draznin, M. B. (2010). Managing the adolescent athlete with type 1 diabetes mellitus. *Pediatric Clinics of North America, 57*(3), 829–837. https://doi.org/10.1016/j.pcl.2010.02.003

Harris, G. D., & White, R. D. (2012). Diabetes in the competitive athlete. *Current Sports Medicine Reports, 11*(6), 309–315.

Hornsby, W. G., & Chetlin, R. D. (2005). Management of competitive athletes with diabetes. *Diabetes Spectrum, 18*(2), 102–107.

Horton, W. B., & Subauste, J. S. (2016). Care of the athlete with type 1 diabetes mellitus: A clinical review. *International Journal of Endocrinology & Metabolism, 14*(2), e36091.

MacKnight, J. M., Mistry, D. J., Pastors, J. G., Holmes, V., & Rynders, C. A. (2009). The daily management of athletes with diabetes. *Clinics in Sports Medicine, 28*(3), 479–495.

CHAPTER 15

Allergies and Asthma

VIGNETTE Part One

"Well done, everyone," said Master Philip as he walked through his group of martial artists. It was not a big group, but it had a diverse mixture of participants, from white to blue belts and composed of all ages. It wasn't always like this, but on Saturdays, he liked to open the classes up a little to let groups intermingle and have some fun in group workouts together. It allowed the more advanced to help the lesser advanced and so on.

"Okay, last thing on the agenda today is?" He waited with a grin as some smiled and others groaned. "That's right. The fitness rounds! Rounds of fitness based on your belt. So, it'll be 3 minutes per belt with one1 minute rests in between. Let's start with some pushups, shall we?" He smiled as he walked over to his phone to start the music and timer. Some loved the fitness components, and some hated them, but fitness was an important component of martial arts that he felt some coaches ignored.

"Okay, let's begin!" At that, Philip tapped his phone and away his group went, some working hard and some, well, not so hard, as they progressed through the belt stages. As the group thinned and the higher belts remained, Philip relaxed a little. "Another day in paradise," he thought to himself as he looked out the window to the main high street. It was a sunny May day, and while the Florida heat and humidity were definitely picking up, he loved his job and where he lived.

But Philip's lapse in concentration was quickly brought back to reality by a shout.

"Master!"

He turned quickly to see Petra lying on the floor with her friend Tamarind kneeling beside her.

Forms, Definitions, and Prevalence

Allergies are common in the general population. The Asthma and Allergy Foundation of America (AAFA) estimates that as many as 30% of adults and 40% of children have allergies. An allergy (or allergic reaction) is evident when the immune system in the body overreacts to a substance (otherwise known as an *allergen*) that it perceives as harmful. Allergies are often experienced as a chronic disease in that they last a long time and may occur often.

Allergens are found in certain drugs, food, insects, latex, mold, animals and pets (e.g., dander), and pollen. The latter allergen, pollen, is a common instigator of seasonal allergies, also known as hay fever. Trees, grasses, and weeds release very small grains that can be spread by wind and be airborne. They can then be inhaled by humans. It is common in certain areas with high amounts of certain kinds of plants to see a thin layer of yellowish green pollen covering items, including vehicles and equipment, left outdoors. It is common for weather forecasters and apps, as well as air purifiers, to include a "pollen count" to indicate how much pollen is in the environment. As the pollen count increases, so does the chance of experiencing reactions for those with allergies.

Allergens can enter the body by being inhaled through breathing, ingested through food, injected (e.g., shots, insect bites), or absorbed by the skin (e.g., poison ivy, latex, chemicals). Reactionary symptoms vary widely, and severity depends on a lot of factors, including level of exposure and individual sensitivity. There are eye allergies, skin allergies, nasal allergies (also called rhinitis), and sinus allergies (or sinusitis). Common symptoms include:

- Enhanced mucus production
- Runny nose
- Sneezing
- Itchiness
- Red or watery eyes
- Nasal congestion
- Hives
- Swelling

Some symptoms may be indicative of a very serious reaction, called *anaphylaxis*, which requires immediate medical attention. More intense and serious symptoms can include:

- Vomiting and diarrhea
- Throat swelling

- Wheezing
- Chest tightness
- Shortness of breath
- Feeling of lightheadedness

Allergens can also trigger *asthma*, a condition in which someone's airways swell, narrow, and possibly produce extra mucus (see **Figure 15.1**). The Centers for Disease Control and Prevention (CDC) estimates that as many at 25 million individuals in the United States have asthma. Asthma can be minor or more severe and symptoms can involve:

- Coughing
- Wheezing
- Chest tightness
- Shortness of breath
- Rapid breathing

Similar to how it is with anaphylaxis, there can be severe asthma attacks that require immediate medical attention. Symptoms in these cases may include:

- Rapid and deep movement of ribs and stomach
- Expanded chest that doesn't deflate when exhaling
- Pale or blue coloring in face or lips
- Rapid movement of nostrils

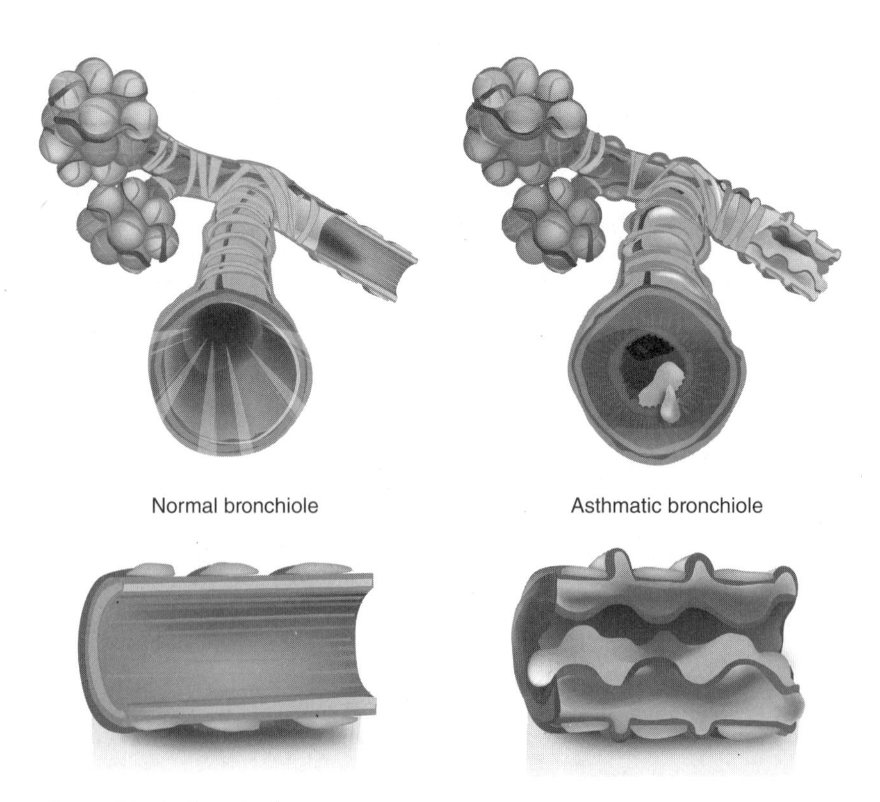

Figure 15.1 Asthmatic airway.

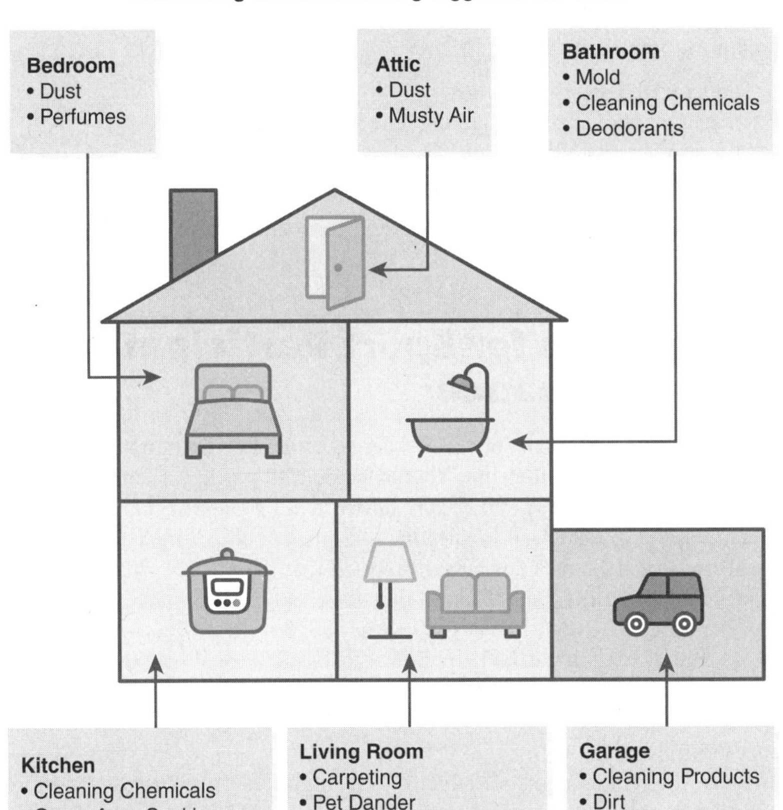

The AAFA publishes a list of the top 100 challenging places in the United States to live with seasonal allergies (see link in resources at the end of this unit). They factor in seasonal pollen counts, local use of allergy medications, and the number of local allergist offices. In 2020, the most challenging city to live in with seasonal allergies was Richmond, Virginia. The AAFA also publishes a list of the most challenging places to live with asthma, not only based upon prevalence of diagnosed asthma but also on the number of hospital visits due to asthma. In 2020, Springfield, Massachusetts, was rated the most challenging place to live with asthma.

How Allergies and Asthma Are Recognized

Allergies and asthma can occur across a lifespan. A child who demonstrates symptoms, including consistent cough or sneezing, rashes or hives, or gets an upset stomach or cramps after certain foods, may have allergies. For proper diagnosis, it is sensible for parents or guardians to consult with an allergist. Tests for allergies may include skin prick or blood tests. If allergies are identified, there are a variety of treatment options, including:

- Reducing and avoiding allergens
- Medicine options (antihistamines, nose sprays, decongestants)
- Immunotherapy (allergy shots)

Early diagnosis and treatment can help improve quality of life for children and their families by reducing symptoms and consequent sick days from school or sports, or other activities that are limited when allergies strike.

Implications for Sport Participation and Performance

According to the American College of Allergy, Asthma & Immunology (ACAAI), athletes with allergies and asthma should be able to participate in any physical activity and sport, *provided that doctor's advice is being followed*. For instance, for asthmatic athletes, use of an inhaler may be prescribed before practice to help control symptoms. Some studies have reported that the rates of asthma and allergies may be higher in athletes than in the general population (e.g., Bonini et al., 2009; Bonini et al., 2015; Boulet & O'Byrne, 2015; Robson-Ansley et al., 2012; Thomas et al., 2010). It can be helpful for coaches to know how these conditions and reactions may impact an athlete's ability to function optimally (at various times of the year and in various locales) but also how to help lessen and help manage symptoms.

Given the requirements for athletes to be outdoors or in spaces (e.g., pools) in which they are exposed to pollen and other forms of allergens, many must deal with allergies and allergic (or asthmatic) reactions. Many of the symptoms of allergies and asthma may directly impact performance, such as when there are respiratory reactions that make aerobic activities difficult. Indirectly, athletes may avoid certain workouts, venues, or intensities in which they are fearful of an allergic or asthmatic reaction.

© backgarden/Shutterstock.

If an athlete discloses allergies or asthma, the coach may inquire if an "action plan" has been submitted to the school medical personnel or administrative office. Coaches could have a copy of an athlete "emergency plan." An example from the ACAAI is offered in **Figure 15.2**.

Anaphylaxis Emergency Action Plan

Patient Name: ______________________________ **Age:** __________

Allergies: ______________________________

Asthma ☐ **Yes** ***(high risk for severe reaction)*** ☐ **No**

Additional health problems besides anaphylaxis: ______________________________

____

Concurrent medications: ______________________________

____

	Symptoms of Anaphylaxis
MOUTH	itching, swelling of lips and/or tongue
THROAT*	itching, tightness/closure, hoarseness
SKIN	itching, hives, redness, swelling
GUT	vomiting, diarrhea, cramps
LUNG*	shortness of breath, cough, wheeze
HEART*	weak pulse, dizziness, passing out

Only a few symptoms may be present. Severity of symptoms can change quickly.
****Some symptoms can be life-threatening. ACT FAST!***

Emergency Action Steps - DO NOT HESITATE TO GIVE EPINEPHRINE!

1. Inject epinephrine in thigh using (check one):

☐ Adrenaclick (0.15 mg) ☐ Adrenaclick (0.3 mg)

☐ Auvi-Q (0.15 mg) ☐ Auvi-Q (0.3 mg)

☐ EpiPen Jr (0.15 mg) ☐ EpiPen (0.3 mg)

Epinephrine Injection, USP Auto-injector- authorized generic
☐ (0.15 mg) ☐ (0.3 mg)

☐ Other (0.15 mg) ☐ Other (0.3 mg)

Specify others: ______________________________

IMPORTANT: ASTHMA INHALERS AND/OR ANTIHISTAMINES CAN'T BE DEPENDED ON IN ANAPHYLAXIS.

2. Call 911 or rescue squad (before calling contact)

3. Emergency contact #1: home__________ **work**__________ **cell**__________

Emergency contact #2: home__________ **work**__________ **cell**__________

Emergency contact #3: home__________ **work**__________ **cell**__________

Comments: ______________________________

____

____
Doctor's Signature/Date/Phone Number

____
Parent's Signature (for individuals under age 18 yrs)/Date

This information is for general purposes and is not intended to replace the advice of a qualified health professional. For more information, visit www.aaaai.org. © 2017 American Academy of Allergy, Asthma & Immunology 4/2017

Figure 15.2 Sample emergency plan.

Reproduced from American Academy of Allergy, Ashtma & Immunology. (2017). *Anaphylaxis emergeny action plan.* http://www.aaaai.org/Aaaai/media/MediaLibrary/PDF%20 Documents/Libraries/Anaphylaxis-Emergency-Action-Plan.pdf

Coaching Techniques and Strategies

While it is beyond the role of most coaches to make specific medical or pharmacologic suggestions or interventions, coaches can help construct a plan to reduce or avoid allergens for their athletes. If athletes demonstrate allergic symptoms in practice and competition and it impacts their performance, the coach may inquire about allergic history and if there are steps that can be taken to help reduce the symptoms. If athletes disclose severe allergies or asthma, the coach may desire to let teammates know how to recognize such symptoms. This may be important in practice scenarios when coaches may not have the athletes in constant view. For example, cross country runners may go out on a trail for a long run, and teammates would be the first point of contact in an emergency. In addition, some practical guidance (from the AAFA) about how to reduce or prevent seasonal allergies:

- Monitor pollen counts through a reliable weather service app.
    - Consider having an array of indoor alternatives for athletes on high pollen days.
- Keep windows closed when indoors.
- Encourage good hygiene after practices, competitions, and at home (shower, shampoo, cleaning nasal passages).
- Encourage regular washing of practice clothing and bedding.
- Seek out medical professionals if symptoms worsen.

In addition, when traveling, coaches can double check that athletes are prepared for trips with medications and food alternatives and help guide them in terms of choices when it comes to eating food in restaurants.

VIGNETTE Part Two

Philip rushed over to where Petra lay.

"What's wrong?" he asked, kneeling beside her. Petra looked panicked and was breathing very rapidly.

"I don't know exactly," Tamarind responded. "One minute she was jogging on the spot and the next she just started breathing really fast until she just collapsed!

Philip took a deep breath and tried not to panic himself. It doesn't matter how much training you do, you are never 100% prepared for an emergency like this.

"Okay. Everyone please move away. Tom, turn off the music. Rachel, call 911 and explain that Tamarind is having difficulty trying to breathe." Philip turned to Tamarind. "Okay, Tamarind, I know this is hard but try to slow down your breathing. You're going to be okay. Do you know what's causing this?"

Tamarind nodded in-between breaths.

"Okay, good. Is it asthma or something like that?"

Again, she nodded.

"Okay, keep trying to breathe slowly. Do you know where your inhaler is?"

Panic set in when Philip asked her that and he realized the problem. The inhaler wasn't there, and Tamarind knew, which made her panic even more. He didn't even know she had asthma, and hard exercise combined with the Florida heat, humidity, and spring pollen count, made the situation a perfect storm.

"How had I not known she had asthma? How could I not have known?" he asked himself again. What could have easily been prevented had become a medical emergency because of his lack of care. "This can't be happening," he groaned internally, praying that the emergency team would arrive soon. "This. Can't. Be. Happening."

Additional Resources

- American College of Asthma, Allergies, & Immunology (ACAAI): www.acaai.org
- The ACAAI has an online "symptom test" and allergist locater tool (https://acaai.org/allergies/who-has-allergies/children-allergies) if coaches find themselves wanting to refer an athlete.
- Asthma and Allergy Foundation of America (AAFA): www.aafa.org
- The Centers for Disease Control and Prevention (CDC): https://www.cdc.gov/asthma

Summary

- An allergy is apparent when the immune system in the body overreacts to a substance (otherwise known as an *allergen*) it perceives as harmful.
- Asthma is a condition in which someone's airways swell, narrow, and possibly produce extra mucus. It can be triggered by allergens.
- With medical guidance, individuals with allergies and asthma should be able to participate in most sports.
- Some sport environments or tasks can be more "triggering" than others for allergic reactions and asthma attacks.
- Coaches should not only know how these conditions and reactions may impact an athlete's ability to function optimally (at various times of the year and in various locales) but also how to help lessen and help manage symptoms.
- Coaches can promote and encourage a variety of techniques to prevent or reduce allergen exposure.
- Coaches can be knowledgeable about the action plan in the event of an emergency.

Questions for Consideration

1. How common are allergies?
2. T/F: Some research suggests allergies and asthma may be more prevalent in athletes than in the general population.
3. How would you suspect that an athlete potentially has allergies or asthma?
4. What are some ideas and strategies to reduce allergen exposure for an athlete who has intense allergic reactions?
5. Prior to an out-of-town competition, what are some items you could cover with an athlete (who has allergies or asthma) to ensure they are prepared?

References

Bonini, M., Braido, F., Baiardini, I., Del Giacco, S., Gramiccioni, C., Manara, M., Tagliapietra, G., Scardigno, A., Sargentini, V., Brozzi, M., Rasi, G., & Bonini, S. (2009). AQUA©: Allergy questionnaire for athletes: Development and validation. *Medicine & Science in Sports & Exercise, 41*(5), 1034–1041.

Bonini, M., Gramiccioni, C., Fioretti, D., Ruckert, B., Rinaldi, M., Akdis, C., Todaro, A., Palange, P., Carlsen, K. H., Pelliccia, A., Rasi, G., & Bonini, S. (2015). Asthma, allergy and the Olympics: A 12-year survey in elite athletes. *Current Opinion in Allergy & Clinical Immunology, 15*(2), 184–192.

Boulet, L. P., & O'Byrne, P. M. (2015). Asthma and exercise-induced bronchoconstriction in athletes. *The New England Journal of Medicine, 372*(7), 641–648.

Robson-Ansley, P., Howatson, G., Tallent, J., Mitcheson, K., Walshe, I., Toms, C., Du Toit, G., Smith, M., & Ansley, L. (2012). Prevalence of allergy and upper respiratory tract symptoms in runners of the London marathon. *Medicine & Science in Sports & Exercise, 44*(6), 999–1004.

Thomas, S., Wolfarth, B., Wittmer, C., Nowak, D., & Radon, K. (2010). Self-reported asthma and allergies in top athletes compared to the general population - results of the German part of the GA²LEN-Olympic study 2008. *Allergy, Asthma & Clinical Immunology, 6*(1), 31.

CHAPTER 16

Mental Health, Trauma, and Sleep

VIGNETTE Part One

"10 PM. Lights out guys," Coach Laith Judson said quietly to the room. "Big day tomorrow."

"Got it Coach," said Fabian, one of the star swimmers in the program. Laith waited for a few moments while Laith and his roommate Kale settled before switching off the light and shutting the door. He moved on to the next room down the hotel hallway and the next until he had spoken to the entire team of boys. Some were ready for bed, while others had clearly not expected his knock. His assistant coach, Wendy Roche, did the same for those rooms occupied by the female team.

He headed back to his own room, which he shared with his volunteer assistant coach, Tim Godfrey. They and Wendy had been together for 3 years now and had developed a promising men's and women's college Division III program. Yes, there were hiccups like any program, but the team had been improving and had put themselves into a good position to medal at the conference championships, and maybe even win. He could dream after all.

After a short conversation with Tim and preparing himself for bed, Laith said goodnight to Tim and lights were out by 10:30 PM. Tomorrow was going to be quite a day and all Laith could do was hope that all of the preparation, the details, the training, the nutrition, the mental conditioning, and everything else would pay dividends. Although a swim coach could make small adjustments on the day for a team, team success in the pool largely depended on the work put in prior to the performance.

"Well," Laith thought to himself in the still of the night, "Murphy's Law states that 'whatever can go wrong, will go wrong.' So, what's going to go wrong? Hopefully, we thought of everything." With that final thought, the mental exhaustion of being responsible for a group of young athletes on the road caught up with him and he drifted off to dramatic dreams.

Mental Health

Mental health, like physical health, is not just the absence of disease or disorder. It should be fostered and monitored. There are best practices when it comes to maintaining physical health and there are ways to help support mental health through daily practices and routines. Mental and physical health can work to support one another. A Latin phrase—from which the sport world now has the brand name *ASICS*—is "anima sana in corpore sana," which means *sound mind in a sound body*. Coaches are often able to support physical and mental health for their teams and athletes. They can also be part of a "pathway" for health support.

Children or adolescents experiencing distress may demonstrate it in ways different from adults. What is more, childhood and adolescence are marked by such continual physical, social, intellectual, emotional, and athletic changes and development, it can be difficult to ascertain what is to be expected and what is not. In some cases, changes in mood or behavior are temporary and normal. In other cases, they may be signs of something much more serious that needs attention. Below are some warning signs of poor mental health.

- Persistent sadness
- Withdrawal from social situations or activities they used to enjoy
- Outbursts and irritability
- Behavior that seems out-of-place or out-of-control
- Changes in mood
- Changes in diet
- Difficulty sleeping
- Fatigue
- Frequent headaches, stomachaches, or other pain
- Difficulty concentrating
- Changes in academic or athletic performance
- Changes in school or sport participation or attendance

A unit on mental health in this book was needed for multiple reasons. First, there are many symptoms associated with changes in mental health that may appear the same or similar to many of the signs and symptoms of some hidden disabilities and conditions. In some cases, an underlying mental health issue could be present, which brings up a second reason to cover mental health: coaches may often be in an excellent position to recognize the symptoms and be part of a "pathway" to communication and support. Third, there is also inclusion of important resources for help. Along those lines, some researchers tested a mental health in sport action plan for coaches (Sebbens, Hassmén, Crisp, & Wensley, 2016). The steps in this plan can be remembered as the 4 Rs:

- Recognize
- Reach out
- Refer
- Remain supportive

The *recognize* phase places importance on coaches knowing more about mental health, including prevalence in the general population as well as signs of certain mental health problems, including depressive symptoms, anxiety, and suicidal thoughts. To better recognize mental health in athletes, coaches can understand the ways in which sport can introduce unique or additional pressures or stress to athletes, which can be additional risk factors.

In the *reach out* phase, coaches attempt to start private conversations with individuals with whom they are concerned. Coaches can focus on describing the observable behaviors that they have noticed are troubling and which have caused concern (not trying to make any informal diagnosis). If athletes disclose what is going on with them, coaches should use *active listening* skills as they listen to the athlete. Some basic tips on this type of listening:

- Paraphrase what the speaker is saying from time to time—it helps the listener understand and shows the speaker that the listener is trying to grasp the situation.
- When appropriate, ask questions to get the person to elaborate.
- Use body language that indicates that you are listening: Make eye contact, stay relaxed, and avoid expressions or gestures that may indicate frustration or disapproval.
- Avoid judgement—just try to understand the situation.
- Avoid giving advice—that can come later.

While listening, coaches may communicate those feelings and stress are normal, and there are people who can help us learn tools to cope better. With this information, coaches can better understand if there is time to work out a plan, or help is needed right away. In urgent cases, some help may be needed, although there is time to work out a plan. In emergency cases, help is needed right away.

In the *refer* phase, coaches help the athletes connect with a medical or counseling professional, whether at the institution (like a school counselor, counseling center) or in the community. Spending time finding local mental health professionals and being aware of mental health hotlines can help get information to athletes quickly.

An important question is when is it time to refer? A useful analogy may be with physical injury. There are many aches and pains that are typical for athletes that they are somewhat accustomed to dealing with ... whether during certain times of the year or after certain events. For these types of injuries, from experience, the athlete may have the perspective, knowledge, resources, and support to handle it. However, sometimes physical injuries get more serious. Some of the questions that come along with it and may prompt a doctor's visit are:

- Is the injury completely new to me?
- Is the injury one that I have experienced before, but it's getting more intense this time?
- Is the injury one that I have experienced before, but the ways I managed it before aren't working to make it better this time?
- Is the injury just not going away the way I expected it to?
- Is the pain from this injury too much for me to handle without help right away?

The same general idea can be applied to mental health by replacing the term "injury" with the term(s) "stress" or "emotions." If the answers to one or more of the above is "yes," it may be useful to refer the athlete for more help. In cases in which the pain is too much and help is needed right away, or if the individual poses an immediate danger to themselves or others (an emergency situation), the coach can call 911. It can be helpful for coaches to have an updated referral list with contact information for professionals who can help, including medical doctors, psychologists or counselors, and nutritionists. There are also crisis hotlines (see the "hotlines" section at the end of this chapter). In 2020, the *National Suicide Hotline Designation Act* was signed into law. It is not scheduled to take effect until some point in 2022, although when it does, people can call 988 for mental health emergencies and support.

Finally, to *remain supportive*, coaches can follow up with individuals afterwards to offer emotional and practical support, again using active listening techniques. In some cases, the first referral may not have worked out, and more help to find a better fit may be helpful or necessary. Together, coaches can be an incredibly protective figure for athletes who may be experiencing significant stress and mental health challenges (Schinke et al., 2018).

Trauma

Mental health symptoms may be caused by any number of biological or social factors, including traumatic circumstances. Broadly, *trauma* is an emotional response to a terrible event, or set of events. Some potential traumatic events include:

- Bullying
- Community violence
- Racism
- Physical abuse and violence
- Sexual abuse
- Neglect
- Substance use in a family
- Accidents
- Natural disasters

- Medical issues
- Loss and grief

The traumatic event(s) may be direct in that it threatens the person, or it can be an event that was witnessed. In some cases, coaches may be aware of factors that may prompt a traumatic response, such as a natural disaster (e.g., hurricane, tornado, wildfire) that causes displacement from the home, or community violence, which may occur in the immediate area or is highly publicized in the media. Coaches should be aware that traumatic events could also originate in the team environment (e.g., bullying, racism, harassment).

Racial trauma—or *race-based stress*—is emotional injury from singular or repeated acts of discrimination, racism, or hate crimes (Comas-Díaz et al., 2019; Helms et al., 2010). This form of trauma can again be experienced directly (e.g., from teammates, spectators, opponents) or indirectly (e.g., witnessing it between others; seeing cases in the media). As authority figures in sport contexts, coaches should clearly and adamantly demonstrate that they are opposed to racist and discriminatory language and behaviors. If discriminatory or racist behaviors occur within the team environment, coaches should act immediately. The *Rise to Win* program (link offered in resources at the end of the chapter) has a variety of resources and activities that may be helpful for coaches to have discussions about racism and generate ideas to reduce problematic attitudes and behaviors on their team. For instance, teammates could be given time to get to know one another on an individual basis, which can help reduce prejudicial thoughts and attitudes.

Coaches may also be able to recognize potentially traumatic issues such as neglect (e.g., basic needs are not being met) or substance use (particularly if family members do so in public situations). Coaches may also be aware that some populations may be at higher risk for trauma, including those from families with substance abuse, experiencing economic distress or homelessness, and military affiliation. In addition, children with intellectual or developmental disabilities as well as youth identifying as LGBTQIA+ may be at higher risk for bullying.

In many other cases, coaches would not necessarily have direct knowledge of the traumatic event unless it was disclosed. Because not all individuals experience stress following a traumatic event, it may be particularly difficult to detect sometimes. Trauma can also be *acute* (as a one-time event) or *chronic* (multiple instances happen over time). In any case, children deal with the event(s) by developing emotional and behavioral responses that may be apparent to others and that may also interfere with relationships and friendships, interests, school, and sports. Some of these symptoms may look like other symptoms discussed throughout this book for various issues including:

- Intense and ongoing emotional upset
- Depressive symptoms or anxiety
- Behavioral changes
- Difficulties with self-regulation
- Problems interacting with others
- Loss of previously acquired skills
- Attention and academic difficulties
- Nightmares
- Difficulty sleeping

- Loss of appetite
- Aches and pains

Other stress responses to trauma may seem less obvious, such as changes that are apparent in a hyperfocus upon tasks, or being hypersensitive to feedback, correction, or criticism. Many coaches may have a rapport with their athletes where the athlete feels comfortable confiding in the coach about the trauma that the athlete is experiencing. Additionally, coaches may be able to observe changes in behavior or mood that may have been brought on by traumatic experiences. According to the National Child Traumatic Stress Initiative (NCTSI), coaches—like parents and guardians—can reassure individuals experiencing traumatic stress by doing the following:

- Ensure that they are safe and that you, along with other trusted adults, can take steps to ensure their safety.
- Explain to them that they did not cause the traumatic event to occur and should not blame themselves.
- Be supportive and patient.

Sleep

Sometimes, the physical or mental symptoms or changes that coaches observe may be due to lack of proper sleep. The demands for quality sleep may be higher for athletes given their need to expend large volumes of physical energy over the course of a season, as well as the need to properly recover from workouts, injuries, and travel. The amount and quality of sleep contributes a lot to such recovery, as well as mental alertness and health. Many large athletic organizations, such as the NCAA and International Olympic Committee, have published consensus statements in which they cite the importance of healthy sleep for athletes in relation to their athletic performance and mental health (Kroshus et al., 2019; Reardon et al., 2019).

Briefly, sleep should take individuals through various stages, with sleep getting increasingly deeper from stage 1 of light sleep where someone can still be easily awoken through stage 3 of deep sleep (Tubbs et al., 2019). In this stage, muscles are very relaxed, and this is when most muscular recovery occurs. It is also when most growth hormone is released. In the rapid eye movement (REM) stage the blood flow in the brain is very active and this stage is important for memory and emotion formation. Dreams and nightmares occur in this stage. So, adequate, extended periods of sleep permit adequate movement in and out of these stages and help promote growth, recovery, and performance for athletes.

The amount of sleep recommended for a healthy adult is about 7 hours, but other groups, including children, adolescents, and athletes may need more (Hirshkowitz et al., 2015). Sleep problems can be prevalent in athletes. Some of the sleep problems can be serious, such as insomnia and sleep apnea. These may require professional intervention from a sleep specialist.

Many times, though, sleep problems may be a case of insufficient sleep, which can occur for a variety of reasons (stress, disruptions in schedule)

(Tubbs et al., 2019). Insufficient sleep can impact performance in many ways, including negatively impacting performance, and can be a risk factor for poor mental health (Charest & Grandner, 2020).

In cases of insufficient sleep, some basic sleep hygiene and management may be helpful. Some items coaches can consider:

- Educate athletes on the connection between good sleep and sport performance.
- Help athletes prioritize sleep—recognize that athletes often also juggle school, jobs, and relationships in their daily lives, so they may not get enough sleep at night.
- Encourage napping (where possible).
    - Strategic or "power" naps—30 minutes or fewer may be most helpful.
    - Naps that are excessively long can interfere with night sleeping.
    - The best time for strategic naps may be after lunch and into the early afternoon.
- Encourage athletes to extend and "bank" sleep. Encourage more sleep in the weeks leading up to important competitions.
- Encourage athletes to avoid situations or stimuli that present risks to sleep.
- Have fixed routines surrounding the evening and transition to sleep.
- Dim lights and unplug electronics during transition periods.

Some of these suggestions may be easier than others, and changes usually work best when implemented gradually. Sleep is an issue that coaches can educate and promote for all athletes, and if certain athletes at certain times are having sleep problems, the coach may be able to permit more time for that athlete to extend their sleep.

In some cases, the sleep problems seem particularly intense, such as when it seems to be coinciding with extreme sleepiness during the day, observable changes in mood or ability to handle day-to-day tasks (in or out of sport), and if it otherwise appears that the athlete cannot manage it on their own. In such cases, the coach may reach out and help connect the athlete with a qualified professional as they would with mental health concerns.

VIGNETTE Part Two

The day brought forth sunshine but Laith, his assistants, and his team would see none of it as they headed out in the early morning to the natatorium. It was the big day, and while there was some excited chatter on the charter bus, there were clearly some who were not yet awake. Laith did not think much of it, and once again tried to anticipate anything that might impede their path to their best performance.

All went according to plan until his team hit the pool. Some of them, particularly Fabian, Kale, Raymond, and John looked very sluggish in warmups. Laith pulled them aside.

"Hey, what's going on?"

"What do you mean, Coach?" asked Raymond.

"Why are you four so sluggish looking? Why did you look so sleepy on the bus? Where's the normal energy I see from my leaders and seniors? What's going on?"

Furtive looks passed between the four.

"I said WHAT'S GOING ON?" Laith said a little louder this time.

There was more shuffling and fidgeting, but this time, Laith waited in that uncomfortable silence that forces a response. Finally, Fabian broke.

"Sorry, Coach."

"What do you mean 'Sorry'?"

"Well, we never get to play with each other much so we wanted to have a tournament."

"What on earth are you talking about?"

"DeathStar," Kale blurted out.

"What?"

"DeathStar," Kale said again. "You know. The online gaming platform that everyone's playing. It's awesome and we never get to play together. So last night we wanted to. And, well, when we got into it and started winning and it just kind of got out of hand."

"So, let me get this straight. After lights out you all got out your pocket whatevers and played computer games with each other?"

"Uh, yeah." Again, the shuffling, fidgeting, and avoiding of eye contact with Laith was palpable.

Laith took a moment. "So when did you go to sleep?"

"Uh, like 2 AM" responded Kale.

"Uh huh. So when did you REALLY go to bed?"

"Uh, more like 4 AM."

Laith closed his eyes and sighed deeply. All the work. All the training. All the effort. All those best laid plans laid to waste by four young men who valued a few hours of gaming over a title. Where had he gone wrong?

Additional Resources

Mental Health and Trauma Resources and Hotlines

- Black Mental Health Alliance: https://blackmentalhealth.com/
- Latinx Therapy: https://latinxtherapy.com/
- National Suicide Prevention Lifeline 24/7 confidential hotline: 800-273-8255
- Substance Abuse and Mental Health Services Administration (SAMHSA) 24/7 confidential hotline: 800-662-HELP
- National Alliance on Mental Illness (NAMI): https://www.nami.org/
- National Collegiate Athletic Association (NCAA). Mental health best practices: https://www.ncaa.org/sport-science-institute/mental-health-best-practices
- National Child Traumatic Stress Network (NCTSN): https://www.nctsn.org/
- Substance Abuse and Mental Health Services Administration: https://www.samhsa.gov/child-trauma/about-nctsi
- National Suicide Prevention Lifeline: https://suicidepreventionlifeline.org/
- Return on Inclusion: https://www.roinclusion.com/
- Rise to Win: https://risetowin.org/index.html
- South Asian Mental Health Initiative & Network: https://samhin.org/
- Substance Abuse and Mental Health Services Administration (SAMHSA): https://www.samhsa.gov/find-help/national-helpline
- Ted Talks to help understand racism: https://www.ted.com/playlists/250/talks_to_help_you_understand_r
- Therapy for Black Girls: https://therapyforblackgirls.com/

Sleep Resources

- Elite Rest: https://www.elite-rest.com/
- National Collegiate Athletic Association (NCAA): https://www.ncaa.org/sport-science-institute/topics/sleep-and-wellness-educational-resources
- National Sleep Foundation: https://www.thensf.org/

Summary

- Indicators of poor mental health and stress reactions to trauma can mirror some of the signs of hidden disabilities and sensory conditions.
- Coaches may often be in an excellent position to recognize the symptoms and be part of a "pathway" to communication and support for mental health and trauma.
- Coaches can follow the 4 Rs:
  - Recognize
  - Reach out
  - Refer
  - Remain supportive
- Issues (including mental health changes) can also be related to difficulties with sleeping.
- Coaches may be able to educate athletes about the importance of self-care and encourage good sleep hygiene and discipline.

Questions for Consideration

1. What does ASICS mean and why is it relevant to this chapter?
2. What do the 4 Rs stand for and what do they mean from the perspective of a coach?
3. What are the basics tips for active listening?
4. How does physical injury assessment apply to mental health assessments?
5. Sleep is perhaps vastly underappreciated for its many positive effects on performance. In your experience, what inhibits coaches and athletes from getting adequate sleep? Using the content of the chapter, what steps could you implement to address a general lack of sleep in athletics?

References

Charest, J., & Grandner, M. A. (2020). Sleep and athletic performance: Impacts on physical performance, mental performance, injury risk and recovery, and mental health. *Sleep Medicine Clinics, 15*(1), 41–57.

Comas-Díaz, L., Hall, G. N., & Neville, H. A. (2019). Racial trauma: Theory, research, and healing: Introduction to the special issue. *American Psychologist, 74*(1), 1–5.

Helms, J. E., Nicolas, G., & Green, C. E. (2010). Racism and ethnoviolence as trauma: Enhancing professional training. *Traumatology, 16*(4), 53–62. https://doi.org/10.1177/1534765610389595

Hirshkowitz, M., Whiton, K., Albert, S. M., Alessi, C., Bruni, O., DonCarlos, L., Hazen, N., Herman, J., Adams Hillard, P. J., Katz, E. S., Kheirandish-Gozal, L., Neubauer, D. N, O'Donnell, A. E., Ohayon, M., Peever, J., Rawding R., Sachdeva, R. C., Setters, B., Vitiello, M. V., & Ware, J. C. (2015). National Sleep Foundation's updated sleep duration recommendations: Final report. *Sleep Health, 1*(4), 233–243.

Kroshus, E., Wagner, J., Wyrick, D., Athey, A., Bell, L., Benjamin, H. J., Grandner, M. A., Kline, C. E., Mohler, J. M., Prichard, J. R., Watson, N. F., & Hainline, B. (2019). Wake up call for collegiate athlete sleep: Narrative review and consensus recommendations from the NCAA Interassociation Task Force on Sleep and Wellness. *British Journal of Sports Medicine, 53*(12), 731–736.

Rancourt, D., Brauer, A., Palermo, M., Choquette, E. M., & Stanley, C. (2020). Response to Tomalski et al. (2019): Recommendations for adapting a comprehensive athlete mental health screening program for broad dissemination. *Journal of Sport Psychology in Action, 11*(1), 57–67.

Reardon, C. L., Hainline, B., Aron, C. M., Baron, D., Baum, A. L., Bindra, A., Budgett, R., Campriani, N., Castaldelli-Maia, J. M., Currie, A., Derevensky, J. L., Glick, I. D., Gorczynski, P., Gouttebarge, V., Grandner, M. A., Han, D. H., McDuff, D., Mountjoy, M., Polat, A., . . . Engebretsen, L. (2019). Mental health in elite athletes: International Olympic Committee consensus statement (2019). *British Journal of Sports Medicine, 53*(11), 667–699.

Schinke, R. J., Stambulova, N. B., Si, G., & Moore, Z. (2018). International society of sport psychology position stand: Athletes' mental health, performance, and development. *International Journal of Sport and Exercise Psychology, 16*(6), 622–639.

Sebbens, J., Hassmén, P., Crisp, D., & Wensley, K. (2016). Mental health in sport (MHS): Improving the early intervention knowledge and confidence of elite sport staff. *Frontiers in Psychology, 7*, 911.

Tubbs, A. S., Dollish, H. K., Fernandez, F., & Grandner, M. A. (2019). The basics of sleep physiology and behavior. In M. A. Grandner (Ed.), *Sleep and Health* (pp. 3–10). Academic Press.

Index

Note: Page numbers followed by *f* and *t* indicate figures and tables, respectively.

C

D

F

H

I

J

K

L

M

N

O

P

R

S

T

Z